<u>Book</u>

Bethany Joy Lenz

Other Chapters of an Inspiring Life and Dinner for Vampires

Copyright © 2024
All rights reserved

The content of this book may not be reproduced, duplicated, or transmitted without the author's or publisher's express written permission. Under no circumstances will the publisher or author be held liable or legally responsible for any damages, reparation, or monetary loss caused by the information contained in this book, whether directly or indirectly.

Legal Notice:

This publication is copyrighted. It is strictly for personal use only. You may not change, distribute, sell, use, quote, or paraphrase any part of this book without the author's or publisher's permission.

Disclaimer Notice:

Please note that the information in this document is for educational and entertainment purposes. Every effort has been made to present accurate, up-to-date, reliable, and comprehensive information. There are no express or implied warranties. Readers understand that the author is not providing legal, financial, medical, or professional advice. This book's content was compiled from a variety of sources. Please seek the advice of a licensed professional before attempting any of the techniques described in this book. By reading this document, the reader agrees that the author is not liable for any direct or indirect losses incurred due to using the information contained within this document, including, but not limited to, errors, omissions, or inaccuracies.

TABLE OF CONTENTS

PROLOGUE

PART ONE

Chapter One

Chapter Two

Chapter Three

Chapter Four

Chapter Five

Chapter Six

Chapter Seven

Chapter Eight

Chapter Nine

Chapter Ten

Chapter Eleven

PART TWO

Chapter Twelve

Chapter Thirteen

Chapter Fourteen

Chapter Fifteen

Chapter Sixteen

Chapter Seventeen

Chapter Eighteen

Chapter Nineteen

Chapter Twenty

Chapter Twenty-One

Chapter Twenty-Two

PART THREE

Chapter Twenty-Three

Chapter Twenty-Four

PROLOGUE

"I do not want to do this anymore. Maybe we should separate for a while."

When I said that, he was facing me from across the hotel room. He became quiet. Tense. I had not used the term "divorce," but it was near enough. His chest moved in weak breaths. He blinked several times.

"And what about Rosie?" he said. "Who does she go with?"

Rosie. She rustled on the bed between us, still in her car seat, next to the baggage we needed to pack for our flight back to Idaho in a few hours. There she lay, eleven months old and already in turmoil. Her evenings were filled with the sounds of her parents' heated disagreements, slamming doors, and Mom wailing in closets. Furthermore, she took six months to correctly latch on to my nipple because she was born with a tongue-tie, so her introduction to sustenance was a mother weeping in anguish, generally screaming into a pillow so she wouldn't be disturbed while I pushed through, bleeding into the milk. Yes, there were plenty of walks in the sunshine, naps on our chests, and clutching her father's thumbs while he cooed over her and blew raspberries on her stomach. It was her favorite. He could always make her laugh by doing this. She would look up at us, but it was we who were fascinated by everything she did. There were pleasant times. However, most of the time, we lived in a chaotic world.

I said gently, "Well..." "I mean..." "I am nursing her, so..."

He shook his head and took a quick breath before picking up a sweater, balling it up, and throwing it at me with a roar.

It was only a sweatshirt. Before that, it was just a toy. Only one book. Only a cellphone. Only potted plants. Only a vintage rolling metal laundry basket collided with a wall, ricocheted to the floor, and scared our brave five-pound Yorkshire dog so much that he crap himself exactly where he stood. He had merely hurt his hand by punching holes in numerous of our walls and doors. A sweater was essentially nothing.

My husband's father had pushed his three kids from a young age to vent their wrath against women on the drywall and furniture, and he set the example himself. "Right in front of the woman, if needed," Les would provide instruction, "so she can see how passionate you are about her and see how controlled you are to not harm her in spite of the fact that she makes you so angry." And boy, did I make my spouse mad. Everything I did, said, and thought seemed to reflect my very existence.

He was especially unhappy with me lately because we were about to go back to Los Angeles, where we had met and spent the previous few days looking for a place to live and meeting new acting managers. Since marriage, I'd shared my time between our family's home base in Idaho and the Wilmington, North Carolina, set of the hit TV series One Tree Hill, where I played Haley James Scott for nine seasons. The millions I earned benefited not only us, but also the extended Family's numerous ventures, which included a motel, a restaurant, and, most importantly, a ministry. Now that the play had ended, I'd have to go back to auditioning, which didn't happen in Idaho. He abhorred the idea of leaving his family.

That afternoon in our West Hollywood hotel, he had been ranting at me for nearly an hour, which was normal. I was fatigued. I'd been exhausted for years. The therapist I had started seeing about this time advised me to set some boundaries to help me manage these emotional storms. "Start with something simple," she had said. "Take violence as an example. Physical aggression around you is not tolerated. Ever." Then I said this to him: "If you throw something across the room again, I'm going to immediately remove myself and Rosie from that situation and we can try talking again the next day."

He did not like it. I believe he said, "I don't agree to that."

In the split second after he flung the hoodie, I had to decide whether to enforce my boundaries or not. I debated letting it go and waiting till he threw something heavy. I did not want to make matters worse. I could simply let it go for now, and we could discuss it later. I was looking for a method to live independently for a few months anyway. Go to counseling together and attempt to start over—just get away from his family and their controlling behavior for a bit. This concept threw me off, thinking of them as his family rather than ours. That was an unusual and unexpected emotion. More startling than the thought itself was how correct it seemed. But I didn't have time to think about what that meant. If I stayed, I might bring all of this up again, along with the possibility of separation. Don't do it now, Joy. It was only a sweatshirt.

I just gazed down at my daughter's face for the first time since the

conflict started, and everything inside me shifted. Her eyes looked strange. They were constantly deep and bright, as if small stars had landed in them. People regularly observed, laughing, that she seemed to be peering into their soul. But at that moment, her large, lovely chocolate eyes appeared dismal, nearly lifeless. I realized she had merely sat in the room for an hour, letting her father's venom wash over us. Isn't that how plants die in fifth-grade science experiments: isolate them in a room and yell at them?
I took up Rosie and cradled her against my chest. She was limp and looked quite forlorn. Perhaps I was projecting. Maybe it was just my imagination. Maybe God was present, as I'd known Him to be many times before, and He was allowing me to see myself from a higher perspective. Whatever it was, my body became frigid. And then it got very, very hot.
I'd carried her for nine months, read parenting books, and delivered her myself after a twenty-hour labor, reaching down and pulling my baby out of me in the final moments. I breastfed her several times per day despite the anguish of her inability to latch. I woke up with her in the middle of the night and accompanied her to work at five a.m. I prayed for her, fed her, changed her, drove her to her doctor's visits, and spoke positively about her on a daily basis—I did everything a mother does. But I believe it was in that moment—seeing her light go out, knowing why, and knowing I was the only one who could do anything—that I truly became a mother. That silly hoodie became the heaviest thing he'd ever thrown.
I began to assemble my belongings. "I told you if you threw another thing I was going to leave with her for the night." I expressed it pragmatically, holding out hope that he would apologize.
I didn't even notice him moving. He appeared unexpectedly. As I sat on the bed, he leant in, his arms blocking me on either side, and his breath was hot in my face.
"If you go," he yelled, "I'll call a lawyer and take her from you. I will battle for custody, and I will win. I'll take. Her. "Away from you."
My heart was a kick drum. He was convinced that the girl he knew would not depart. The girl he knew would stay because, despite the constant battle and depression, she hadn't left. The girl he knew was determined to make the marriage work. She was attempting to be a Godly and submissive wife. She knew she was selfish, and all she needed was more healing—more surrender. She knew, deep down,

how much he'd given up for her, how patient he was with her brokenness. The girl he knew needed him.

I also know that girl. I'd been living in her skin for ten years, convinced she was the true me. But where was the girl I was before? Prior to the downward slide into accepting abuse and relinquishing my autonomy not only to him, but also to our Family—no, his Family. "No, to a..." I wasn't quite prepared to admit it. I felt much more afraid to use that term than "divorce." My estranged parents, former acquaintances, and coworkers had been using this phrase for years. The word that further alienated me from them, but which I began to suspect was true.

He stood up, still glowering at me, and walked into the bathroom, slamming the door and turning on the shower. I was fortunate that he banked on me becoming paralyzed with dread, but I knew my time was limited. I hurriedly loaded Rosie into her car seat, grabbed my suitcase, and ran to the rental car. Instead of traveling to the airport, I let him fly home without us, while Rosie and I stayed with some old friends for the next week. He pleaded via text before doubling down on scolding me for my insubordination, selfishness, and heartlessness. Again, standard. Then he turned cold. His texts were almost robotic, which pushed me even further away.

After a week spent with old friends and phone talks with my therapist and parents, I was reminded of the other girl I used to be. I was reminded that I was still her, and I finally reached a point where I could admit it.

I was in a cult. And I needed to get out.

PART ONE

CHAPTER ONE

My first memory of the American Christian-culture Crock-Pot in which I was baked was around 1985: I was four years old, sitting in the middle of the back seat bench in my parents' black Harvester Scout, my tan, string bean legs stuck to the vinyl as I endured the seventeen-hour drive from south Florida to central Texas. With the metal seat belt tight around my small waist—booster seats were a thing of the past—I repeatedly pulled on the rope that protruded from the spine of my favorite doll, Melody.

Melody was a Christian equivalent of Teddy Ruxpin or Cabbage Patch Kids. She had only one song. Pull the string, and she'll sing, Hosanna! Hosanna! Shout to God in triumph! Clap your hands, all ye people, and worship God! She arose from the thriving business of catering to the charismatic evangelical movement that erupted in the United States in the 1980s: Christian rock music, cartoon Bibles, tacky cross jewelry, and Lord-praising dolls.

My parents had left the Jesus Revolution hippy era and were now at the forefront of this new movement, having met and graduated from one of the country's largest charismatic Bible colleges. According to the account, Dad stepped out of the gym after losing a pickup basketball game and noticed Mom in the bursar's queue, registering for a class. He jumped into his '64 Mustang and dashed back to his hostel to get the only cash he had—five dollars—so he could join her in line and have an excuse to speak with her. Mom (with her below-the-knee skirt) grinned at Dad standing behind her. He may have had a haircut to conform to the conservative university standards, but he remained a hippie at heart. Dad noticed her Bambi-like face and exclaimed, "You look like you have stars in your eyes," and three years later I was born in Florida. We lived in the Coconut Creek home of my father's off-the-boat Australian grandfather, which had an orange tree and Pompano Beach in the backyard. The heat was oppressive, but the water was my playground.

Dad had a teaching degree, but there were no open opportunities nearby, so he worked wherever he could: painting houses, mowing lawns, and grudgingly taking a perilous job as a prison guard. Mom painted artwork onto white baby onesies and sold them for money. They eventually accepted a position as "house parents" in a facility for troubled teenage females. It was free housing and board, and they viewed it as a ministry opportunity. This lasted for nearly a year, until one of the girls threatened to cook me. Mom got us out of there within a week, and they were determined to improve our lives.

Dad had been submitting résumés all over the country and had landed a position as a high school teacher at a famous Christian school in Texas. Mom was also hired as the new secretary to the president of the largest Christian music label in the country. So Dad sold the Mustang and purchased the more family-friendly Scout. We packed up and left for Dallas, where there was equally scorching heat but no ocean. Early on, I had frequent dreams about the swaying citrus groves and palm trees we'd left behind. I felt safe amidst the damp gloom. To this day, I would rather be hot than cold, and the smell of salt and oranges brings me great comfort.

But life moves on, and so did we. A small apartment on the outskirts of town became home. I received a free ride to the private school because my father taught there, but finding friends proved difficult. It wasn't only the isolation of being the only child. I felt a profound disconnect between my life—riding to school in a truck with broken heat while warming my hands on the cigarette lighter or "World's Best Dad" coffee mug I'd made him in kindergarten—and the other kids'—who arrived at school in Cadillac Escalades with new Magical Mansion Barbie Dreamhouses." My social life consisted mostly of the singing Melody doll and our new cocker spaniel puppy, so I was overjoyed to learn that Jesus would be my constant companion.

Dinnertime prayers were common in our household, as were regular references to the moral counsel provided by Proverbs, Psalms, and parables, as well as everyday discussions about God. Dad possessed a New King James Bible wrapped in leather so thick it belonged on a saddle. He read it with a highlighter and pen nearby, meticulously marking every inch of the margin.

One night at my bedside, Dad finished reading to me from 1 Peter about Jesus taking our sins on himself, closed that leather Bible on his lap, and asked, "Do you know that God is so perfect that anything imperfect is destroyed just by being near Him? "Like a light being turned on in a dark room." He then switched the switch on the wall.

I dropped my head beneath the blankets and giggled.

He smiled. "Look around!" Do you see any darkness?

I looked out and shook my head.

"Where'd it go?" he inquired.

"The light ate it up!" "I said."
"That's right," he remarked, tipping his head back as he always did when he was happy. "This is what God does for us. As long as we keep Him turned on, He eats up all the nasty stuff."
It was straightforward, I understood it, and I eventually embraced my parents' faith.

My parents' new jobs did not last. Over the next eight years, we'd relocate to four different locations in Texas. This meant that I attended four different elementary schools and struggled to retain friendships. To add to the solitude, my parents' stress grew with each job shift and new housing. Loud conversations, chilly rooms, and slammed doors. Because of this volatility, continuously moving schools, and untreated ADHD, I was a lousy student—fidgety and usually daydreaming, unable to complete my homework properly. I attempted to make it fun for myself in every way I could, such as using different colored pens, providing more answers to multiple-choice questions, and creating drawings rather than writing sentences. My professors were fatigued and upset, but fortunately for me, both of my parents were excellent encouragers of creativity. They realized all I needed was to be in an environment that would help me turn my deficiencies into strengths. When I was seven, Mom took me to a small theatre in Arlington, Texas, where I was cast as a munchkin in The Wizard of Oz.
Perhaps it was inevitable that I would become a performer. My family had a lengthy history in the performing arts. My great-grandmother on my mother's side ran away as a teenager to join the circus, finally ending up in vaudeville. My father's parents, Doris and George, were also entertainers. She was a choir director and regional stage actor, while he was a Broadway regular, having appeared in the original productions of South Pacific, Wish You Were Here, and Carousel, as well as serving as stage manager for many more. In the attic of her New Jersey house, Grandma Doris possessed boxes—like BUH-AHH-XES—of playbills from musicals they were in, as well as original cast records, newspaper clippings, and handwritten letters from Broadway superstars like as Shirley Booth and Joshua Logan. My family has a strong scrapbooking game. According to family legend, one day James Garner and Grandpa George were in an alley smoking a cigarette half past the end of a matinee, and Garner said,

"Everybody's calling me to go out to Hollywood, but I don't know if I could leave the theatre." Grandpa George said, "Garner, if you don't get out of this rathole I will personally kick your ass," followed by an apparently convincing argument that led to James Garner packing his bags to try his luck in Hollywood, where

Further research reveals that James Garner never worked on Broadway as a young man. So, either his name got mixed up as the story was passed down, or Grandpa George was just full of shit—which, given that he hooked up with a dancer from The Jackie Gleason Show and left Doris, my six-year-old father, and his nine-year-old sister with severe physical disabilities, is probably the correct answer.

I hardly knew him, but Grandma Doris was a symphony of music and warmth. When we visited her in Jersey, I would steal a Werther's butterscotch from the crystal candy dish on the upright piano, pull the cord hanging from the upstairs hallway ceiling, climb the creaking stairs, and spend hours in her attic. That highest point of the home featured a solitary, dusty window and innumerable saved props and costumes from earlier shows, allowing me to get lost playing dress-up and immersing myself in family history. I felt that I could learn more about who I was there, and I wished for a family connection.

The Arlington Community Theatre gave me my first sense of truly belonging somewhere. The creative arts school has dozens of rooms for rehearsals, costume creation, set design, and dance and voice lessons. People were everywhere, fighting to hear one other over the noises of singing, clacking tap shoes, blaring stereos, and instrument practices. I was energized by the odors of paint, sawdust, Aqua Net, and Pond's cold cream; hot lights and pure sweat.

On the enormous auditorium stage during the first night of The Wizard of Oz, I was meant to pass over a prop to Dorothy and realized my character would loathe Toto, so I recoiled and held my nose. The dog required a bath regardless. I heard a ripple of laughter and knew I had influenced the emotional experience of a large group of people. After a few more performances on stage, I learned I could forget about my issues at home and school and become whomever I wanted. On top of that, I was welcomed! My idiosyncrasies, such as spontaneous singing, copying Lucille Ball, and daydreaming, got me into trouble at school, but they served me well in acting. I went on to star in all of the traditional local theatre productions, including Annie, Gypsy, To Kill a Mockingbird, and Peter Pan. I was becoming a vital member of a community, which meant everything to me. At the age of twelve, I received a highlighted review in the Dallas Morning News—my first newspaper clipping! Next, I was cast in my first on-screen part, as the lead actress in a Christian film with a huge costumed songbook singer. Think of Barney the purple dinosaur, but with a blue church hymnal. Psalty's Salvation Celebration is easily found online. You are welcome.

Soon after making the transition from stage to screen, I enrolled in another new institution, this time devoted to television and cinema, and my first trip to Los Angeles was planned. Mom and I spent a week in a furnished Hollywood apartment, attending every audition we could find. Apparently, I was receiving positive comments from casting agents, and when I reached the coveted final round of the Mickey Mouse Club tryouts (the same year Britney and Justin were cast), I overheard Mom telling Dad over the phone, "She might really have a shot at this!"

It seemed plain to me what I was supposed to do with my life. It was also evident to Grandma Doris. During one of my last visits to see her, after she was diagnosed with late-stage cancer, she gave me some job advise, referring to me as a mentor rather than a grandma.

"It's a hard life to be an actor," she said as I applied her eyeshadow. Carole King played in the background of the stereo. Doesn't anyone stay in one spot anymore? A short, layered wig lay beside us on the kitchen table. We'd put it on last. "It's difficult to be rejected and continually compete. But there is nothing more wonderful than being able to share stories. I couldn't imagine doing anything else. It made me so happy." She paused for a bit, allowing me to apply her favorite glossy mauve lipstick from a silver tube. It would be great to see your face at my door. She squeezed her lips together. "I have many regrets in life, but I don't regret one second I spent onstage." She embraced me close to her warm chest and stared into my eyes. "Sing your heart out, youngster. One day, your name will be in lights. "I truly believe that, but you're so far away..."

When she died, she left the New Jersey house to her father. Deep down, however, I felt it was also her present to me: bringing me closer to New York City and exposing me to actual training, casting, and Broadway.

We left the South and moved into the two-bedroom home where my father grew up. Dad took a position as an adventure coordinator/ropes course director at a mental health facility, which essentially meant he was doing group therapy on an adult playground. Mom had a job selling beige business phones with built-in shoulder rests—to whom I'm not sure, but I was constantly finding boxes of phones about the home. With my huge teeth, Texas twang, and icy blonde hair, I enrolled in the same public school that Dad attended and made exactly zero friends, at the request of the queen bee, who thought being pleasant and southern was strange. Using my acting abilities, I immediately shed the accent and became a "Jersey girl" for a while, until I realized that the facade of brown lip liner, flannel shirts, and feeble efforts to smoke cigarettes to impress said queen bee would only get me so far. After taking an introductory French class, I decided that I felt more like a "French girl" inside, so I spelled my name "Joie" and surrounded myself with everything French: Catherine Deneuve and Juliette Binoche movie posters taped to my bedroom walls, Les Mis and Serge Gainsbourg on my CD player, and a constant rotation of berets. This also did not lead to new friendships.

I felt more alone than ever and missed my Texas theatre community. Even though Mom drove me to New York City several times a week for dance and vocal lessons and auditions, it was still an hour and a half trip on a good day, and too far away for social gatherings. My parents and I started going to a local church that featured a Friday night youth group meeting, which was essentially a club for tweens and teens. They insisted on my attendance in order to keep me socialized, and that first night changed my life forever.

I entered into a large recreation room with fluorescent lights and around fifteen children running around. I felt at ease onstage yet uneasy amid a crowd. I had no idea how to stand or hold my arms, who to talk to, or what to talk about. Then, just as I was about to stuff my face with cheap pizza and hide in a corner to die, I heard a loud chuckle from across the room. A dishwater blond lad with oceanic blue eyes lassoed my vision. He approached and introduced himself in an unusually deep voice for his age. And the only thought on my mind was that I was going to marry you.

His parents were highly regarded in the church and community. The family consisted of two boys, a middle sister, and a Weimaraner. They were pleasant and friendly, and they all looked like they had just gotten off bicycles in Nantucket. He and I quickly became close buddies. We talked for hours every night, with me using the shoulder rest on our beige coil-corded phone in the living room. We both adored Jesus and the Dave Matthews Band. We shared the same sense of humor. And he was the only other person I knew who despised cats. Since I no longer belonged to a theatre community, I decided he was where I belonged.

I began traveling more for acting assignments, and while it kept me away from Blue Eyes, I enjoyed it. Mom would fly with me to Los Angeles for weeks at a time to screen test or film a pilot. I'd play Paul Sorvino's kid, James Franco's sister, or Ben Foster and Gabrielle Union's best friend. The latter was a comedy pilot set in the 1970s for CBS that we were all sure would get picked up, but Fox released its fall lineup first, and CBS didn't want to compete with That '70s Show. Though my pilots were not picked up, my name was spreading, and I was being invited to luxury mansion parties where I recognized almost everyone I saw. It was wonderful to be one of the cool people, given how awkward I used to feel at school, but I never forgot what my father told me about keeping God's light on. I was alert to the underlying ego and darkness that seemed to accompany these kind of Hollywood surroundings, where no one batted an eyelid if I was handed a drink at the bar and cocaine was passed around on trays. I didn't dare tell my parents about these stories, but I did tell Blue Eyes, a like-minded person who shared my desire to make God proud.

Talking long distance every night was too expensive during those excursions, and email wasn't widely available (much alone laptops), so he and I would write letters. We wrote to each other about anything, including receipts and old homework. He once mailed me a note written on a large piece of wallpaper he had ripped from under the bed frame of a hotel when he was on vacation with his family. In school, we passed notes indefinitely. I'm surprised the tenth-grade Spanish class radiator didn't collapse from all the paper we put within, hiding notes for each other to discover later. In the summers, we'd drive in his little Volkswagen Jetta to his family's Jersey lake house (not Nantucket, but nonetheless wonderful), lay on the pier with our legs hanging over the lake, and discuss all of life's major themes.

He and his family were a burrow I wanted to hide in while my parents fought to save their broken marriage. They had broken up once when I was younger but reconciled for my sake. The years that followed were riddled with animosity and passive-aggressive language. The full-fledged arguments would take place behind thin walls and closed doors, from which my mother would emerge with barely veiled composure. If I ever questioned, "What is wrong?"" or "Are you all okay?""Her answer was usually the same: upturned lips. "Everything is fine!""

My mother had not acquired the family's acting gene, and in her attempts to protect me, she accidentally led me down a rabbit hole of questioning my reality—a trait that was valuable to me as an actress but equally useful to anyone who tried to exploit me.

When I needed to get away, Blue Eyes was there to listen and console. However, I refused to cry in front of him. There was no way I was going to fall into a pool of tears for him to clean up. That is not what his cheerleading girlfriend did. Blue Eyes was, of course, the school's great athlete, and he was on and off again with the head cheerleader, as if that cliché need their assistance. There I was, penning songs and poetry for him, weeping nightly into my old cocker spaniel's neck, and patiently waiting for him to realize he loved me. I felt my singing would win him over, so I joined the church's worship team. Perhaps acting success would impress him. That year, I booked a few national ads and a Stephen King film titled Thinner. I was brought in as Monica Keena's understudy for The Devil's Advocate due to a scheduling difficulty, and I walked on set with the incredibly nice and tall Keanu Reeves—only to have Monica arrive after rehearsal, which devastated me. Later, I earned a minor role on the daytime serial show Guiding Light as the teenage clone—yes, clone—of popular character Reva Shayne. But evidently, none of that compared to doing cartwheels on the sidelines of a football game.

Then, one Saturday morning, as I was blow-drying my hair before going to Blue Eyes' place to rent a movie and hang out, my father asked me to come into the living room. Mom sat on a chair, weeping. They told me they were getting divorced. Mom began to explain, confess, apologize, and rationalize. After ten minutes, I asked if I could go finish blow-drying my hair."

They exchanged looks before releasing me.

Later, while exploring the French film area at Blockbuster Video, I nonchalantly told Blue Eyes, "So, my parents are getting a divorce." When the words left my mouth, my face turned heated, my throat burned, and tears welled up in my eyes. I am sure he had no idea what to do, just like I did. He was simply a dumb teenager, like myself. He tsked and replied, "Ah, J, I'm sorry to hear that. You okay?"

I wasn't feeling well, but I said yes nonetheless, frightened that he would think of me as high-maintenance. I also refused to cry when I was pulled off the worship team a few weeks later, which my mother had to tell me while driving home from church.

"Apparently the pastors decided it's too confusing for you to be leading worship onstage while you're on a soap opera."

"Confusing? What's so confusing about it?"

"Because soaps are 'tawdry,' which makes the church look like they endorse that kind of 'behavior.'"

Mom was enraged, and I felt my own humiliation and wrath rise up. "Do they know what acting is? I am only sharing a story. And my character doesn't even do any of that."

"It's not just that… With your dad and I divorcing, they just think it's complicated for the congregation."

I was quiet.

"It's fine," she replied. "They were fortunate to have you. Idiots."

While I appreciated my mother's loyalty and fierce protection—whether in this case, defending me against bullying stage moms who felt I was a threat to their daughters, or demanding that the conservative middle school English teacher accept my Broadway research paper (first denied as "too secular" a topic), her overbearingness also worked against me.

Mom and I had no buffer after Dad moved out and remarried during my senior year. One night, my mother and I were having one of our usual shouting matches. We did not curse (decent Christians do not curse). I never said "I hate you," but I felt it frequently. But that night, she had chased me around the home, even into the bathroom. I said, "Fuck." She slapped me. I screamed in her face, "Leave me alone!!!" Then I grabbed my keys and dashed out to my car—an Eddie Bauer-edition Ford Bronco that I still wish I had, despite its faulty air conditioning.

She was on my heels, but I was able to sneak inside and lock all of the doors. With wild eyes, she pounded on the windows and tried the handle. Then she stood in front of the car, crossed her arms, and looked at me like, "Ha." Gotcha.

I felt she was so foolish. Sit on the hood of the automobile if you don't want me to drive off.

I feigned to put the Bronco in reverse without actually shifting gears. I looked behind me as if I was about to back up, and she hurried to the back of the car to try to block me on that side. As soon as she moved, I slipped out.

I determined to get away from her as quickly as possible, and she seemed to agree. Mom connected with someone from California online. When I graduated after six months, they decided to marry immediately. He flew out the week before my commencement ceremony to assist her with packing.

"This is unbelievable," she grumbled to him on the day they loaded boxes onto the moving truck, the day after my graduation. She was looking at me, sitting in the middle of the living room, designing a frock using the design software that came with our new Apple computer, thanks to the money from my "sinful" Guiding Light job. I was attempting to take my mind off Blue Eyes, to whom I'd bid a hasty goodbye at his graduation celebration by slathering my lips in Bath & Body Works wild-berry-flavored lip balm and eventually mustering the confidence to kiss him. It was little more than a peck, but I knew it would be the last time we saw each other that summer, since he was traveling with his family before attending a midwestern college. So I had to take a chance. He grinned and said thank you before we were swept up in the rush of yearbook signings and congrats. Then he pretended nothing happened.

"Joy, could you please get off the computer and help me? I'm relocating across the nation!"

"No, thanks," I answered calmly.

California attempted to calm her down. He was constantly attempting to calm her down. "Let her do her thing." If she wants to be disrespectful, she has graduated and is now an adult; it is her choice." Is this what I was? An adult? Thank you for visiting our education factory. Please toss this hat in the air and go live your own life. I looked around our vacant house. Dad's home. Doris's home. I pressed my toes firmly into the faded brown carpet.

"Well, you need to be out by Wednesday for the new owners," she remarked, walking to the vehicle with a package containing a beige phone cord dangling from the bottom. "And you'd better get started, because I won't be here to clean up after you."
It was time for me to look for a new place to belong.

I had previously considered moving to Manhattan, hoping to finally realize the destiny Grandma Doris had for me, and my choice was cemented when I received a call from my manager informing me that Guiding Light wanted to hire me as a series regular. So, at the age of eighteen, and following a vacation to Paris in which I was disappointed not to be captivated by a debonair bohemian as I'd been promised by years of watching French cinema, I moved into a little Union Square flat. I didn't know anyone, but I immediately made friends with the Guiding Light cast and other performers I'd come across at tryouts. I also made pals in the local music scene. I had broadened my songwriting beyond ballads for Blue Eyes and formed a band that performed around town, including iconic local venues such as CBGB and the Bitter End. I landed a role as Mary Tyler Moore's daughter in a made-for-TV movie and began auditioning for Broadway on a regular basis. I was establishing a real life in New York, but my deepest friendships were formed in church.
An acquaintance introduced me to a little church that gathered in the residence of a sweet pastoral couple from South Africa. The Bible studies we held were similar to others I had attended in my life: personal, relaxed, and full of interest. Our South African pastors, for example, encouraged us to attend other churches on occasion in order to diversify our spiritual diet. I began attending Redeemer Presbyterian Church, which was pastored by Reverend Dr. Timothy Keller, whose 2023 New York Times obituary characterized him as a "pioneering evangelist" who was well admired for his brilliance and intellectual engagement in contemporary culture. Personally, I didn't think of him as an evangelist. Tim was a theologian who insisted on reason as the foundation for faith, which I like since it reminded me of how my father would push me to think. Tim and his wife, Kathy, founded the Upper East Side church in 1989, and the congregation grew to include thousands of New Yorkers from many backgrounds. There, I met Camille, an auburn-haired Brit who was also an actor. We'd met in so many casting rooms that seeing her at Redeemer

cemented our friendship. She had grown up Catholic and was curious about "all the other options." We had plenty of chat because I was also fascinated. Camille was the first actor friend with whom I did not feel competitive; all I wanted was for her to win. And so, when she told me a few months into our friendship that she was relocating to Los Angeles to look for employment, I was both sad and supportive.

I never envisioned leaving New York City, especially after discovering such supportive networks in my spiritual and professional lives. I loved living there, the creative pulp that seemed to surge into my veins every time I stepped outside—the feeling of everyone piled on top of each other, getting in each other's way, holding each other up, and spurring one another forward. I felt fearless there, and most importantly, I felt like I belonged.

With Blue Eyes, things looked even more hopeful! He came to visit one weekend, and after a long day of touring and sexual tension, he stopped me by a streetlamp near Lincoln Center, leaned in, and kissed me. I was confident that this would be the key to unlocking all of the love we had been keeping back. Everything would fall into place now: marriage, a home, children, a wonderful life, and eternal love. However, once he returned to school, we were back where we had been. So, as expected, I returned to waiting for him to come around.

When my Guiding Light contract expired, I chose not to renew. I wanted to advance in my career. Staying in Manhattan for another year, I came close to landing roles in scores of major studio films but never got the job. It was rejection after rejection, but I was determined to realize my ambition. So, when my bank account began to run dangerously low, I did what my parents usually did when money was tight: I hit the road.

CHAPTER TWO

I had gotten a feel of LA's peculiar vibes on my high school trips, but living there full-time was even stranger. There was no sense of community. I had no idea how to get anyplace in the city because it was so spread out. I wanted to enjoy the sunshine, so I foolishly purchased a stick shift convertible Miata and drove through traffic in fourth gear until my joints swelled. I had a strange job at a Beverly Hills florist, where some dumb soul put me in charge of the register before I realized there was a word for dyslexia with numbers. (It's "dyscalculia," by the way.) I soon booked guest appearances on a couple TV shows, but life in LA was all about ego and rivalry. Everything felt like a fight, and I felt quite alone, especially after leaving my community in New York. My mother and I's relationship remained difficult, so despite the fact that we now lived in the same state, we didn't see each other often and spoke on the phone occasionally. I communicated more with my father, who was still in New Jersey, but he was busy with his new family.

Camille and my new roommate, Mina, whom I'd met through a New York-based actress buddy, were my only friends. "She's an actress and a Christian, and you're both romantics," he told her. Our first meeting occurred when she invited me to the TV studio where they were filming a network legal drama in which she was a series regular. I'd filmed a few pilots but hadn't spent much time in a studio like this. Walking through the hallways seeking for Mina's dressing room and seeing name after familiar name lined the walls inspired me. Deep down, I heard the echo of Grandma Doris' promise to me: that I'd soon see my name on one of these doors as well.

The emotion did not stay long. When I got to Mina's dressing room, the door was ajar, and I lost all confidence the instant I knocked and she turned to look at me. If this was the type of beauty required to make it in Hollywood, I didn't have a chance. This woman should have been fought over by Trojans and Greeks, and I was an alley cat, still scraping dumpster greens out of my paw. According to a mutual friend, Mina was ten years older than me. There was no way this woman was a year away from turning thirty.

"You made it!" she exclaimed, running a hand that had previously held cigarettes for magazine advertisements through her slightly limp, coffee-colored hair. I was relieved that my hair was thicker, because I had to take my victories where they came under such difficult conditions.

She opened her arms to hug me, but as she approached, I noticed her makeup was smeared with tears. Then I saw the cardboard box.

"It's kind of a weird day," she added. "I recently found that I was let go from my contract. "I'm packing up my belongings."

"I'm very sorry," I said. "If it's a bad time, we can totally reschedule."

"No," she replied. "I'm delighted you're here. I am pleased to have the companionship. I feel as if I've been expelled from the kingdom. "Everybody is avoiding me." An insecure giggle erupted from her pillow lips, and she wiped her eyes. Despite my fury at God for making her look like way, I resolved to forgive Him.

Mina had also forgiven God for the current affliction. As we spent the next half hour packing her boxes, she described how, despite her disappointment, she found solace in the knowing that this was definitely part of God's plan for her.

"I only became a Christian last year," she explained. "I grew up Catholic, but, you know…" She flicked both hands in front of her, as if to clear the air. "I met an actor who was on the studio lot filming a movie. His name is Harker Van Hewitt. "Do you know him?"

I knew Harker because he was a rising movie star whose acting abilities were as unique as his name. Fellow performers usually have an idea of who among them is on the rise. "Yeah, he's fantastic!"

"Oh, Joy, he's so intelligent and so humble. We began having fantastic debates about Jesus and religious history. I'm not sure, but the Lord just kind of came alive for me."

"Are you dating him?" I inquired.

"Oh, no," she replied. "He is much younger than me. "He is your age."

I wondered whether she had considered it, judging by the way she blushed and how swiftly she responded to their age gap.

"He's quite talented. And his older brother, Abe, has a fantastic band. It resembles indie jazz rock. "Like Dave Matthews."

"I love Dave Matthews!" I murmured, cringing slightly inside as I remembered Blue Eyes. "And I also play music."

"You should definitely meet them," Mina replied, pulling down an award from the now-bare shelf next to her mirror. "Actually, they hold a Saturday night Bible study at their home. Have you found a church here yet?"

I shake my head. "I haven't even found a regular grocery store yet," I admitted.

"This Bible study has sort of taken the place of church for me," Mina was saying. "I just feel so close and connected to everyone. Coming from Catholic churches that are quite rigid and official, this is just so different."

She halted, noticing the trophy in her palm, which she was wrapping in newspaper.

"I can't believe I have to start looking for another job all of a sudden," she told me. Then she smirked. "Isn't this funny? After I became a Christian, my life began to fall apart."

I remembered a conversation with my father in which he highlighted a fundamental element of our faith: "Jesus never claimed life would be easy. In fact, His own life and death would demonstrate this. But He promised to stay with us through it all and give us peace."

I repeated this to Mina, who grinned and closed the cardboard.

"That is very true," she remarked. She took a deep breath.

A few weeks later, Mina encouraged me to move into the spare bedroom of her Beverly Hills condo and assist with the rent now that she was unemployed. Her auditions become fewer and fewer. She may have appeared much younger than thirty, but casting directors could tell by her credits how long she'd been in the industry. And Hollywood is not nice to women after their twenties. While her career was steadily declining, I was beginning to have more success, landing guest appearances on shows such as Felicity and The Guardian. I knew Mina was a good friend when, instead of resenting me, she remained helpful and encouraging. It was the same dynamic I had with Camille, whom I was still close to but didn't see very frequently, given how busy we both were and how difficult it was to navigate traffic.

Most nights, we'd stay up late chatting about boys, which was the only thing we spoke about other than God. Our mutual buddy was correct: Mina and I are both romantics. We went on and on about our unrequited love. Blue Eyes was soon off to law school (of course he was), so we didn't communicate as frequently as we used to—but I remained his first call for dating advise. Mina's name was, as expected, Harker.

"Ten years isn't that big of a difference," I told myself. "I mean, it feels like it now, but it won't when he's thirty-five and you're forty-five."

"Well, technically I'd be forty-four."

"Yeah," I replied. "It's not even a full decade."

"It's not just that," Mina replied. "He recently got engaged to a girl in Idaho. That is where he and his family originally came from."

Mina kept trying to push her emotions aside. One evening, she claimed that they were a "transference"—that Harker guiding her to a spiritual awakening made her feel closer to him than she was.

"I guess that makes sense," I answered. "It still sucks when someone doesn't love you back. "I am sorry."

I remained in bed that night, thinking about Blue Eyes and wondering if my feelings for him were comparable. For so long, he had provided a safe haven for me in times of distress. Perhaps it was not true love after all. Infatuation? For eight years? Was this possible? As I drifted off, wondering what love was, I envisioned his enormous chuckle, which bounced around inside of my body. He stood by the lake with a bare chest and damp, tanned skin. He was tying a rope around his hand and dragging the boat into the pier. He kissed me clumsily in Lincoln Center. Perfect, small white teeth rubbing against mine. He represented salt and oranges, family, and memories in high school corridors and on Manhattan corners. He was everything I missed and made me feel at home. What was I doing out here in Los Angeles? Where did I even belong?

I fell asleep to the sound of automobiles whizzing by on Olympic Boulevard, trying to mislead my head into believing it was the ocean.

My cellphone kept ringing. The sunshine shone through my linen curtains. I hadn't slept well, and now my phone wouldn't stop ringing. I stumbled up to it.

Mom.

"Hey, everything okay?"

"Turn on the TV," she ordered bluntly.

"Why? What's—"

"Just turn on the TV."

Mina's modest square television was located in the center of the living room, inside a massive oak cabinet. I pressed the remote and watched for a few seconds, my mind trying to make sense of the immediate mayhem. Manhattan. Black smoke was rising. Sirens. People are yelling. Ash is everywhere. Just as I started to realize what I was watching, an airplane crashed into the second tower.

For the next several September days, I didn't leave the apartment, not even my bed. Everyone I knew in New York was safe, but I couldn't stop feeling sad for the city I loved and the friends who had lost loved ones. I did not know how to move. I was helpless, unable to connect, and unclear how to grieve. New York seemed like home, and I just wanted to return.

At first, Mina gave me some space. Then, late on Saturday afternoon, she knocked and opened my bedroom door. I didn't realize how much I needed a breath of beauty until she leaned against my doorframe in a bedazzled blue velour Juicy Couture tracksuit, her lips frosted with something pink. Again, it was the early 2000s.

"I think it would be good for you to get out," she told me.

I knew she was correct. "Where?" I inquired, groaning. I was not in the mood to go to a club, pub, or even a movie. However, Mina had a different idea.

"Bible study," she explained.

CHAPTER THREE

On Saturday nights, the front door of the Van Hewitt house in North Hollywood remained open, despite the fact that the neighborhood was not very safe. The flat streets provided an easy environment for the homeless to stroll. The grocery stores and gas stations appeared to have been placed on bare corners by a child who enjoyed Monopoly and eventually became a city planner. Traffic raced by at all hours, and this boxy gray house was directly on the main road, separated only by a small plot of grass that served as a yard in LA. I was amazed at how modest the house was given the brothers' fame. I knew Harker had a long number of film credits, and Abe's band was popular enough to plan a small national tour, but I rapidly grew to respect their modesty. This house was the most the family could afford a decade ago, when the two brothers chose to pursue acting and were successful enough that their family migrated to Los Angeles part-time from Idaho. Though they'd done well enough in the years after to renovate, they were pleased with what they had and didn't want the flashiness that distinguished so many individuals in that town. And what the mansion lacked in size and opulence, it made up for with comfort.

This was thanks to the boys' mother, Pamela. She lived with them part-time and worked as an accountant for the boys' father and her husband, Edward. Ed was a physician with a modest private practice. He remained in Idaho but would travel down to Los Angeles on weekends, or Pam would go up. Pam insisted on cleanliness, so there was never a book out of place, no rogue mug half full of tea, always a lit scented candle, and you had to remove your shoes before entering.

The family had formerly been Seventh-day Adventists, but they had become disillusioned with the church and departed a few years ago. For the past year or so, they had been hosting a Bible study group. The majority of the members had met Harker and Abe through the entertainment industry. They weren't great stars, but they were famous enough that, like Mina, who occasionally received autograph requests on the street from visitors, they would not feel at ease being vulnerable in a typical church situation.

That first evening, as well as the following several months of Saturday meetings, played out in the same way. Pam began by hugging everyone who came through the door. She smelt like the inside of my mother's lingerie drawer, with perfume, silk, sweat, and small packets of dried flowers carefully stored inside an oak chest. It was a drawer I surreptitiously opened when Mom was at work, caressing all the delicate textiles and attempting to learn more about becoming a woman. Or maybe I was trying to feel her warmth without risking her displeasure. Now, snuggled into Pam's neck, her unashamed maternal devotion provided me with much-needed comfort.

This hug was followed by eight more with the remainder of the people in the room, because nothing could begin until everyone had received one. By everyone. We hugged hello and goodbye, sometimes for no reason at all. There was a lot of hugging. As an introvert, this was a challenge for me, but what else could I do? Hello, one embrace tonight is plenty for me. The lucky winner is determined by drawing straws. Or we can all simply wave. Want to wave?

We'd mingle for a while, then Abe began strumming his guitar, signaling everyone to take a seat wherever they could find one. I was familiar with this cue. The evangelical Bible study pattern remained consistent throughout, including at my South African pastors' little New York church and my anti-soap opera church in Jersey: arrive, sing, read, talk, pray, and leave.

At the Van Hewitts', I normally sat on the L-shaped couch, but if I arrived late, I ended myself on the floor. We performed a few worship songs as a form of meditation, focusing on God while blocking out the inner noise of distractions or tension. I hadn't realized how much I missed singing until I sat down to worship with this group. Then Abe would open his well-worn Bible and read.

His voice was comforting. You know when you've been in a room with strong overhead lighting for hours and can't figure out why you have a headache, and then someone puts on a dim lamp and your entire body relaxes? Abe was like the low lamp. You nearly forget it's there, but when it appears, you remember how much you needed it. I remembered Dad and his bedtime story about God being a light, which immediately endeared Abe to me as a friend. He had a charming face that matched his inviting presence—his heavy brows were constantly arched over sympathetic green eyes—and was attractive, but he was sometimes overshadowed by his brother.

Harker was born with symmetry and curves fit for billboards. Surprisingly, he also demonstrated a complete lack of vanity—the uncommon individual who goes past a storefront window and isn't inclined to look at their image. Both brothers were pale, like their father, although Ed was shorter. Harker and Abe didn't put much effort into their wardrobes. I anticipated successful young artists to dress in striped Gucci scarves and leather bracelets, but they preferred Kmart t-shirts and thrift shop jeans. The Van Hewitt brothers simply lacked guile. I completely trusted them.

Abe would finish reading, followed by Harker's comments, and we were soon involved in a free-flowing conversation, challenging or encouraging one another. When the discussion seemed to be coming to a close, Ed—when he was in town—would usually lead a closing prayer, his head bobbing involuntarily as he did so. Then, after about an hour, we'd leave, still hugging on the way out.

It was such a pleasure of my week that I invited Camille, who had also missed the camaraderie we shared in New York. Camille and Mina hadn't met yet, but they'd both been hearing me gushing about the other for months. They got along exactly as I expected, soon connecting over being reared Catholic. The three of us, along with the rest of the group—which was small, about fifteen people—were having such meaningful, close interactions on Saturday evenings that it was very easy to fall in step with each other the rest of the week: lunches, running errands, movie nights, phone calls in which we'd pray with each other before a meeting or audition. It felt a lot like life with my church mates in New York.

That was how it went for the first six months or so. Until the night, everything changed.

Mina and I were the last to arrive on Saturday. She opened the door ahead of me, and by the time I walked in, she was already hugging Emily, a tall blonde shot of dopamine who had grown up with the Van Hewitts in Idaho. After her parents divorced, she relocated to Los Angeles with her mother and began working as a freshly promoted talent manager for a large agency. Emily had become one of the "ones to watch" in Hollywood. She held me next, as my name rose over the din.
"Joy!"
Pam, whose voice was constantly lilting, would always greet me across the room with this. She skipped at me and pounced with a tight hug. "We're so glad you're herrrre."
Camille hugged me next. Then there was Ed, who had come to town for the weekend from Idaho. Then I smelled something coming from the kitchen, which was unusual because the Van Hewitts seldom cooked. The fact that they possessed a stove was funny. They had lived their entire lives following a strict Seventh-day Adventist vegan diet. Now that they were bumbling their way out of it, their parquet cabinets were packed with Nutrisystem bars and "rehydrate me" boxes of TV dinners.
"Who is cooking?"I asked.
"Oh, gosh," Ed exclaimed, bouncing on his toes. "Our friends, Les and Marti, are here! "Come on, I will introduce you."
Whatever was cooking had a meaty basis and an overly sweet fragrance that lingered behind my nose, like the lingering flavor after you've vomited. We turned the corner into the kitchen, and I collided into twin lads, perhaps thirteen years old, battling for a Nerf gun. The Barbarians fled without apologies. I looked up to see a few pots spitting on the burner and three fresh faces in the room.
"Hey, this is Joy," Ed said. "She's another one of our precious daughters here."
The young women in the organization had adopted the moniker "precious daughter". I interpreted it as a symbolic act of care. "Brothers and sisters in Christ" was a fairly common expression in the Christian community, so the concept of "spiritual parents" did not appear to be a leap.

I was met with two identically contrite smiles from a slim middle-aged woman and an equally lanky boy of seventeen. I assumed they were mother and son, and the two Barbarians were hers as well. They stood over the sink with perfect posture, matching long legs, twin heads of coarse brown hair, and almond black eyes that resembled mounted taxidermy doe heads. She washed the dishes, while he dried. They stood so close together that their silhouettes resembled a single person. However, it did not appear awkward or strange. Only as if they were always attempting to take up as little room as possible. The woman opened her mouth. A sound similar to "hi" may have squeaked through, but it was drowned out by the room noise and running water. The silent boy waved.
Thank God, someone is waving.
I had no further thoughts about them except that I would not want to have been born with such faces since all of the bones appeared to be slightly out of place, but they came across as decent enough individuals, and I immediately felt terrible for thinking that.
A short red-faced man in his late forties stood behind them, at the small breakfast table, with hair everywhere except the top of his head. His stomach swelled forward beneath apish arms hovering above a Pyrex dish as he massaged salt into a huge flop of pink flesh. There was something intimate and repulsive about seeing his hairy fingers sink into the liquid mass. I must have stared.
"Gotta give it some love before you beat it into submission!" He laughed cheerfully, rubbing the back of his hand across his sweating brow. A steel meat mallet sat nearby, awaiting its turn. "This BBQ recipe has been in my family for many years. You're going to enjoy it.
"Great! I love barbeque!" I murmured, suddenly picturing every brisket I'd ever eaten with man hands all over it before it reached my lips.
"I'd shake your hand, but..."
I laughed. "You're good."
"What was your name again?""
"Joy."
Hello, Joy. I'm Les. "This is my wife, Martine, and my sons..." He continued to speak, but the stink of whatever was simmering on the stove was starting to bother me. The familiar strum of Abe's guitar began, and everyone in the living room behind me became silent.

That night's Bible verse was Ephesians 2:8-9: "For it is by grace you have been saved, through faith—and this is not from yourselves, but is the gift of God—not by works, so that no one can boast."
When Abe finished reading, Harker stated, "When Abe and I were praying about this passage, it felt like the Lord was reminding us of how often we base our worth on what we do—even what we do for God." Almost as if we're trying to impress Him." Harker spoke softly and casually, as he always did. "But that's the very idea of grace. "He's already done everything."
Abe joined in. "I feel like… I think I'm being humble by making all these sacrifices and performing good deeds or whatever, but that's actually pride to think that I could ever do enough to earn God's love or favor."
Les entered the living room, stepping on the carpet with his shoes. There was no empty chair, so Ed scooted onto the floor and offered Les his oak dining room chair, which he gladly took.
"Not to change the subject," Harker remarked, "but I want to make sure you've all met Les, Marti, and their boys. We know them from Idaho. They were able to come down and visit this week. They've been going through a lot of transition. Do you want to talk about it, Les? I didn't mean to put you on the spot.
Harker smiled, and a slot machine pressed WIN.
"Ah, sure!"Les chuckled awkwardly." He moved his weight in the chair, which I worried might buckle beneath him. The Barbarians were distracted at the kitchen table, drawing on a piece of paper. Quiet Boy sat on another chair behind Les, and Martine was at Les' feet, her long legs tucked sideways like a pinup girl.
"Well, I've been pastoring a small church in Washington for the last few years near the Idaho border, where the Van Hewitts are from, and a few months ago Harker got ahold of a tape recording of one of my sermons, and the Lord just really spoke to him through it." Pam and Ed came to see our church and were increasingly involved in the community we established there. Recently, I've been discussing transition with these folks.
His voice grew sadder.
"Unfortunately, we are now dealing with some extremely difficult situations. We're seeing the enemy take advantage of our lovely church community." (Another Christianese term for Satan.) "We really began to see the Holy Spirit act in mighty ways, and there

were just a lot of folks in the congregation who weren't ready to grow. They disliked the discomfort that comes with growth and healing. And it's really awful to see it break apart, but progress is difficult for many individuals. Growing requires a great deal of courage, and not everyone is made out for it.
Martine was looking at the floor, brows lifted, lips tight, and nodding in accord. Quiet Boy stared straight forward, motionless.
"So, unfortunately, we're in the process of leaving our house—the mission home that the church provided for us and where my children grew up. "Well, since we left New York."
Sighs of compassionate disappointment rang throughout the room.
"Are you from New York?"" I inquired, my face beaming.
"Mm-hmm, right before we moved to Washington."
"No way, I just left there. I am very heartbroken right now."
"Yeah, us too. Awful. I mean, with that and the gravity of quitting the church, we needed a break. So it was great when Ed proposed we go to California for some sun and I could meet all of you."
Ed interjected: "Oh, that was Harker's idea, from his generous heart. We cannot take credit."
"Okay, well, you'll have to let me give you credit for your own generosity," he replied, "because you guys have just blown us away." After that, he addressed the crowd: "Pam and Ed have offered their beautiful home in Idaho to me and my family for a year, to live there while we recalibrate and heal and just see what God has next for us."
"So you're going to move to Los Angeles full-time?" Camille questioned Ed.
"No," Ed answered. "I'll still be going back and forth, but Pam and I will move into the apartment above the garage and give Les and his family the house."
"Oh, wows" and "Amazings!"" resonated as everyone focused on Pam and Ed. Ed ignored the attention and raised the corners of his mouth. Pam nestled her neck between her shoulders and smiled impishly.
"So, we're just so thankful and love hearing about the amazing things God is doing here with you guys in Hollywood," replied Les, "and we look forward to praying for you and encouraging you however we can."
Les smiled at me briefly, full of humble optimism.
I felt bad about how I had misjudged him. Here was this beautiful

pastor, doing his hardest to bring a congregation out of the rigid mindset of structure and religion, being persecuted, having his family kicked out of their house, and I was wrinkling my nose at him because of his appearance and whatever was cooking on the stove. I felt quite pretentious.

See, Joy. You never know what others are going through. Thank God for individuals like him. I never want to be afraid to grow. Every second, the world falls apart a little more. I refuse to squander time in dread. I said, "God, don't let me be afraid to grow."

Despite that commitment, I was not about to consume whatever Les had prepared. So I came up with an excuse to leave early. As I was putting on my shoes, Les approached me.

"So you are a New Yorker, right? What are you doing outside?"

"I am an actress. "Like everyone else."

"Had any luck?"

"Well, I was on a soap opera for a couple years in New York, and I've been doing a few guest spots on some good shows out here."

"I would consider that luck. That sounds like a big blessing, too—you must have made enough money from the show to come out here and audition for a living!"

It was uncomfortable to discuss money with a stranger, but he was so nice and so forthright that it almost felt like a challenge. For example, are you grown enough to have an adult conversation about money?

"It wasn't bad," I said, leaving it vague. "But not as good as movies and prime-time television, which is why I moved out here."

"Where's your family?""

"Mom is in San Diego, Dad is in New Jersey."

"Ah. How old were you when they separated? Is this an Ed and Pam situation?"

"No, they divorced when I was sixteen."

"Tough age."

Strangely, I experienced a similar feeling—the same refusal to be high-maintenance that Blue Eyes had always prompted.

"It was okay," I said. "I knew they were miserable, so it was honestly better."

"Did you grow up in the church?"

"I did. They differed depending on where we were.

"Did you move a lot?"

"All the time." Probably destined to be an actor, musician, or circus performer! "You know, always on the road," I said, smiling.
"What church did you attend in New York?"He asked.
"A modest home church—you would never have heard of it. But I paid a visit to Redeemer Presbyterian. a lot on the upper east. Tim Keller is brilliant. "I wish I had gone more often."
"No way!" I used to pastor alongside him before we departed New York."
"You did it!?""
"I am astonished our paths did not intersect!"
I could not believe it. He used to work with the man who had helped shape my faith. It seemed as if God was confirming that I was on the correct track. I immediately assumed this was someone I could trust.
"Well," I replied; "I hope to see you again soon."
"Yes, Joy," Les answered. "You definitely will."

CHAPTER FOUR

"Hand me the hoisin sauce," Les instructed Camille, who was standing near the pantry when Mina and I entered the Van Hewitt home. Les had returned to town and was once again cooking. "Peking duck was my favorite when I was in Japan."
"When did you go to Japan?" I inquired as he leaned in to offer me a half hug with his free hand.
"With the marines."
"Oorah!" Abe said playfully, removing a nude, dried bird from the refrigerator.
Les lifted the sleeve of his t-shirt to reveal a hideous tattoo of a ship, an eagle, and a gun all smashed together above SEMPER FI.
"How long did you serve?" Mina asked.
"Six years," Les explained as he began painting sauce on the wilted creature. "I was the most skilled sniper in the unit. So good, in fact, that they asked me to train the entire platoon when I was still a private first class. Sergeants too!"
Emily hugged me and then kept her face inches away from mine, looming over me with her big smile and bright, wide eyes. "How did it go?" "Are you a cheerleader?"
Earlier that day, I had a screen test for the cheerleading sequel Bring

It On Again.

"I hope so!" I replied. "I think it went well."

I'd been working steadily, including a Coke commercial, guest appearances on several shows, and frequent screen-testing. I even got a couple theatre engagements, which made me quite delighted because LA isn't known for its theatre. Nonetheless, I found myself in Arthur Allan Seidelman's new musical production of The Outsiders, alongside a terrific cast that included Allison Munn, who, by chance, had a recurring part on That '70s Show. (This wasn't the last time we worked together.) Then came the coolest job of all: playing Pinky Tuscadero in Happy Days: A New Musical, directed by Garry Marshall and musically directed by Carole King and Paul Williams (who composed many Carpenters songs). It was an extraordinary opportunity, and it all felt like evidence that moving to Los Angeles was the proper decision. With each passing week, this new group of pals solidified my place here even more. Even Les began to feel like a fixture in our midst. He still resided in Idaho, and while Marti, the Quiet Boy, and the Barbarians were seldom visitors, Les had become so accustomed to the Van Hewitts that he had adopted the same high-back chair for each visit. We appreciated his presence because he was older and a pastor. We were honored that this wise and experienced religious leader decided to meet with a group of random young artists in Los Angeles. None of us saw that he was progressively taking over Harker's and Abe's de facto leadership roles at these gatherings. Neither Harker nor Abe seemed to notice. Or, if they did, they didn't complain when Les started reading the Scripture and sparking the conversation.

Later that evening, after lecturing on Isaiah 43:25 and forgiveness, he leaned forward in his chair, fingertips steepled, his voice easy and welcoming. "No one needs people pointing out where they're failing because they already know," he told me. "You understand what your problems are! Jesus has already addressed those issues concerning ourselves. Consider how you would feel if you forgiven someone you care about for hurting you but they refused to let go. Imagine if Marti taught herself that every time she injured me, it became part of her identity. I have forgiven her! I don't even think about it anymore! But every time she looks in the mirror, she sees only her failures. "Will that strengthen or weaken our relationship?"

"Yeah," "mmm," and "wow" rang out in different tones throughout the crowd.

"This is how it is with God," Les explained. "We must allow God's forgiveness to transform the way we perceive ourselves, revealing the truth of who we truly are as loved and forgiven. This also allows us to speak the truth over each other."

"So, Les," Pam inquired, "how does that look on a practical basis in relationship? Because if the old has passed and the new has arrived"—quoting Scripture was part of Pam's casual vernacular—"how can we still address the rough edges in each other that need to be smoothed for the sake of true relationship?"

"Relationship" was a keyword, alongside "precious daughter" and "enemy." Relationship was everything religion was not, and everything we all desired.

Then Les responded: "You choose to speak the positive truth of someone's identity, no matter how they're behaving."

Emily chimed in. "My brother is always very negative." It's gotten to the point where I can't spend much time with him or even talk to him on the phone since he refuses to be encouraged or made to feel better. So, wouldn't it be crucial for our relationship if I told him the truth? I mean, it's not a nice thing to hear, but if his sister can't tell him, I'm not sure who will."

"Well." Les cleared his throat. "You said 'tell him the truth,' but what is the truth?" That's an excellent example, Emily, because is it true that he is a negative person? Or is that simply how he acts because of the stories he tells himself?"

Emily furrowed her brow, contemplating this.

Les continued: "What I would say is instead of pointing out to him what he already knows—"

"But does he?" Camille interrupted, glancing at Emily.

Les smiled, slightly irritated. Camille didn't appear to notice.

"I know some people that do this, and I'm not sure if they're conscious. I'm not sure if I'm aware of all my own weaknesses.

"Well, let me finish," Les said, bypassing Camille and turning to Emily. "Instead of telling him what he probably already knows about himself, since he lives in that negative self-talk every day, you could say, 'Bro, I just wanted to let you know that I enjoy talking with you. "You are such a positive force in the world."

"I like that," Pam responded. "It's so kind to look past a person's behavior and instead encourage them to become the person God

created them to be." And, Em, I've watched you two grow up. I believe your brother is aware of his own weaknesses.
"But is it kind of—" I cut myself off. After seeing Les' annoyed smile, I became more mindful of not interfering, but now everyone was staring at me. "It may come across as condescending or passive aggressive." I do not know."
Les had grayish eyes. That was the first time I noticed them focusing entirely on me. "It's only passive aggressive if you don't believe it to be true," he told me. Then those gray eyes darted across the room, and his voice increased slightly. His passion was both appealing and inspiring. "Don't let anyone get away with considering themselves as anything less than completely loved and treasured by God. That is our job as believers: to give up our own fleshly reactions to someone's false self." He stared at me again. "We have to stop being selfish."
Is he talking to me? No, he's simply answering the question. Good Lord, the irony! I am so focused on myself that I believe I am being singled out.
The remainder of the room remained silent, processing. I instantly realized that, except for the Van Hewitt lads, Ed and Les, the rest of us were female. Girls, actually.
Harker began spouting Bible verses: "Therefore, each of you must put off falsehood and speak truthfully to your neighbor, for we are all members of the same body." That is Ephesians 4:25. Proverbs 12:17 states, "Whoever speaks the truth gives honest evidence, but a false witness utters deceit." Also, Proverbs 4:25. And Zechariah 8:16. The Bible has numerous allusions to utilizing one's bodily voice to preach truth. He muttered, "Tolstoy said something on this…" before standing up and strolling to the living room bookshelves.
like he searched, Les continued: "Sharing the truth requires guts and, at times, self-control, like in your case with your brother Emily. Don't be angry with him; instead, enjoy the negativity he brings!" He was incredibly engaging. He made this discourse enjoyable. "Now…
"I'll let you in on the real secret sauce—are you ready?" Les smiled. "It works both ways."
He stopped, hoping for some sort of acknowledgement, a "ohh" or "aha," but it didn't come.
Abe ultimately said, "What does that mean?"
"It is not only about what you say. You have the ability to control

what you'receive' from others! Don't let anyone lie about your identity. If someone wants to label you against the loving reality of who you are, you have the right to say, 'I don't accept that.' Do not accept it, regardless of who they are—a stranger or a parent!"

"Okay, Dostoyevsky once said, 'To love someone is to see them as God intended them,'" Harker said from across the room. "Exactly what you are saying, Les. But this is the quote I was thinking of, about truth." He paged through Tolstoy's Wise Thoughts for Every Day. Pages were marked and highlighted. It reminded me of my father's old bible. Harker read aloud. "Every lie is a poison, and there are no innocuous lies. Only truth is secure. Only truth is so certain that I can count on it. "Only truth gives me comfort—it is the one unbreakable diamond."

"Love that, Harker."

Mina, sitting opposite me on the couch, was growing increasingly emotional. Her face was heated, and she was breathing deeply and slowly. I felt sorry for her. After spending so much time with Harker over the last six months, what had begun as an unlikely infatuation had grown into something far more serious. "I think I'm falling in love with him," she told me the night Harker informed that he and his fiancée had chosen a wedding date and that she would be visiting soon. Mina spent the remainder of the night with her head over the toilet. Since losing her job, she had been unable to find acting work. She didn't have any family here, and the group that had once been her safe haven was now her worst source of grief. She was attempting to focus on her relationship with God, but instead she was crying because the sound of Harker's voice tore her heart out with longing.

I reached over and placed my fingers around her ankle, giving her a small "you are not alone" squeeze. Her hand found mine, and it was pleasant to sit like that for a while. I pondered how it felt to have a sister.

Les's voice reminded me that everyone was already praying.

"Father God," he continued, "we simply ask you this week to help us speak only the loving truth over the people in our lives. Our friends and family; the folks we work with. Lord, we will not linger on the negative and will instead see them as you see them: forgiven and free in Christ.

"Yes, Lord," we repeated with sincerity.

Les moved on. "Guys, if you would just stretch your hands out to Joy."

Oh no! What did I do wrong?

"Joy," he replied, "as we're talking about our true identities, I want to put this into practice—can I just share with you who I see you as?"

I felt so embarrassed. "Sure, yeah," I replied.

"I'm envisioning you in a pawn shop, and I just feel like you've been telling yourself for a long time that you're second best."

The room reverberated with "mmms." A lump developed in my throat.

"God sees how hard you work to do the right things and become a decent lady. But He wants you to adore Him with abandon, as a small girl does, for the little girl will empower the woman within you. You are important and beautiful to God. You are His little Princess. You are pure gold! You're not almost there; you're there. "You are not in second place."

The air was dense. The lump in my throat burned. I felt like all of my blood was in my face, causing an endless flow of tears. I was so eager for these words to come true. The Lenz family was broke; we battled, everything went wrong, and nothing good happened to us. I was always playing catch-up, I was always on the verge of landing a terrific job, I was always the runner-up, the greatest friend, the one who fell behind.

His remarks struck my core wound with surgical precision.

How did he know? How did he know?

I felt overwhelmed. I had never been told anything like this in my entire church life.

"Joy, it's time for you to come out of agreement with the idea that you're runner-up and release the spirit of performance-for-love."

Les' easygoing demeanor made everything seem so regular. It felt safe to believe because it wasn't a huge problem. Just readjusting my perspective. Easy. Relief! "Yes" and "Thank you, Jesus" filled the air in the room.

Les put his hand on my shoulder, which felt comfortable. "You do not have to do anything to earn your spot here. "Not with God, not with us."

I broke. A sudden sigh and gasps of a choking sob engulfed my body. Ugh, being so feeble is awful, I thought. All of these folks were watching me cry. Not just crying. They were paying attention to my needs. I was determined not to be needy. Ever. I made certain of that with Blue Eyes. I would not be a burden on anyone. But then a massive wave of relief struck. They recognized my needs and still loved me.

Pam brushed away my tears with a tissue and the kindness I had always longed for and lacked from my mother. "You are so precious, Joy. "We love you."

Emily approached me and said, "Love you, sis."

"Yes, we love you, sis," Mina replied.

That night, I let go of a burden I'd been carrying for a long time, one that had grown day by day, month by month, year by year. For the first time in my life, I didn't need to put on a performance to find my place in the world. I cleaned myself up in the bathroom before we all went into the kitchen to eat. The dinner smelled just as bad as the first time, but I didn't mind. I wasn't going to leave early. I wasn't going to miss a second of this unwavering affection.

CHAPTER FIVE

"What do you mean you're asking God what you should wear before you get dressed in the morning?" Dad enquired on the phone one evening.

"Dad, I believe God cares about every detail of our life. I'm asking God for advice on everything: which auditions to attend, which friends to hang out with at what times, which movies to see, and even my clothing choices. I really believe that if I am going to surrender to Jesus, I must truly surrender."

I shared this with him, hoping he'd be proud of my bold abandonment of selfish ambitions. His reaction wasn't what I expected.

"Do you believe God wants to teach you on what to wear? Didn't He give you the freedom to make such decisions for yourself?"

"Okay, think about it. What if God told a stranger that they'd see a girl in a purple shirt today, and that was the sign they needed? What if I'm supposed to be the girl in the purple shirt, but I never stopped to ask God what I should wear, so that person never sees the sign?"

Silence as he tried to disentangle that. Then he lowered his voice to a calming tone that I recognized all too well. "And how long does it

take you to hear from God about what you'll wear?" he inquired.
This was the hostage-negotiator voice he had developed while working as a mental health counselor after Bible college. Hearing him use this voice on me, as if I were one of those folks who used to sit in his office, left me shaken. Intimidated. Angry. Hurt.
"I guess I get a feeling..."
"What kind of feeling?"
This was now taking on the tone of an interrogation.
"I don't know, like... something can just seem more right than something else."
"And you attribute that feeling to hearing from God?"
That phrase was really weighted for me. "Hearing from God." Every book of the Bible has humans hearing from God. Every church I visited had pastors and members with a "word from the Lord." So, what exactly was my problem? As Les had mentioned, I already knew what my problem was. I was not dedicated enough. I didn't pray properly. Abe and Harker did not do things the same way. They were always studying, discussing, learning, and teaching. I simply wanted to write, sing, sew, paint, and do everything lovely and creative. No surprise I couldn't hear God. I couldn't sit still long enough for Him to speak to me!
That was all about to change, I decided. I was serious, and now I had accountability and comrades to rely on, even if it meant standing up to my father, whom I was afraid to disappoint.
"Joy, where are you getting this stuff?"
"What do you mean?"
"Who—" He halted himself. Next question: "Where did you say you were going to church again?"
"This is a home Bible study. Same like all the other places we went when I was a kid."
"But what church is it affiliated with?"
"It is not. "It's just friends worshiping together."
"But who is leading it, what curriculum are you using?"
I was frustrated. "No one!" I mean, two brothers who are artists founded it. There's also an elderly preacher. But it's only a circle of buddies. "I mean, weren't Jesus' disciples just a bunch of friends?"
"That was a very specific time in history," my dad stated. "And the leader—the rabbi of that group—was literally Jesus."
"Dad, I just want to do things the right way, and I'm seeking God's

wisdom in everything I do."

He exhaled. "That's good, honey." But I think you should be careful not to overspiritualize things. Yes, God is mysterious, but I'm very confident He cares more about your character growth than if you're wearing the appropriate purple shirt."

I could not believe he did not comprehend. I wasn't surprised that my mother was becoming suspicious; anything that kept me from visiting her more frequently had to be a threat. But it saddened me that my father, who was so adventurous that his job title was literally "adventure course director," couldn't be enthused about the spiritual journey I was embarking on. I'd made friends who loved the God he taught me to love, and we were all looking for the same kind of wonderful, wild faith he had in his teens and twenties. Had his faith truly suffered as a result of life's difficulties? Where was his perseverance, patience, and fire? Where is his character development? This was the first time I felt like I knew something about God better than my father did.

That Saturday night, on my way to the Van Hewitt house, I watched LA speed by from the passenger seat of Mina's little black BMW, the last trace of her former success in this place.

"It's so crazy how every time I try to share with my parents what I'm learning and how I'm growing with the Lord right now, they're so resistant!"

"I agreeeee, Joie." Mina did not say anything without emotion. Even a lousy espresso resulted with animated disinterest. "I want to start breaking the generational curses. This is a behavior that has been passed down repeatedly. I'm just finished with it. I'm tired of the enemies trying to undermine our future."

"Right!?"

"Mm-hmm!"

"They just want to stay in their rut, in their safe zone!" I continued. "Even the boundaries I set, like when my mother says anything nasty about me that isn't true to who I am, I say, 'Mom, I just don't receive that,' and she becomes very offended. It's as if she doesn't understand the concept of doing things differently in order to improve and grow."

Mina nodded. "I understand. It only makes me thankful that the Lord is exposing this to us now, while we are still young enough to change direction. And I just want to be so mindful of every decision I make that I don't revert back to my old family habits."

When we got at the house, Les was there, along with the Barbarians. When he spotted me, his face lighted up, and he gave me the customary hug. He could tell I was feeling down. When he inquired what was wrong, I told him about the chat I had earlier with my father. He placed a sympathetic hand on my shoulder.

"Some people just don't have spiritual ears to hear," he told me. "Especially those who are stuck in a religious routine with God. It's difficult to see loved ones resist the motions of the Holy Spirit. I am proud of you, baby girl. At your age, sticking to your guns requires a great deal of fortitude. I honestly think it's pretty wonderful that you're willing to submit your most fundamental decisions to God's will. "God will honor that."

He continued: "And we just get to pray for your dad."

I didn't realize that, for all my concern about the "truth" of my identity, I wasn't practicing (or was encouraged to practice) speaking loving truth to my own family. I suppose that didn't work both ways.

CHAPTER SIX

A few weeks later, Dad traveled out to visit me in Los Angeles for a long weekend, claiming he needed to spend his frequent flier miles before they expired. Camille kindly offered to drive him up from the airport, as I had an audition at the time his aircraft landed. Knock, knock!" she replied, entering our flat. "I got a delivery!" I turned the corner and watched my father enter the front door behind Camille. He was still a hippy, with thinning hair pulled back into a ponytail beneath his baseball cap, beaded cross necklace and sandals, and a duffel bag draped over his shoulder. We hugged. I was a hugger now.

Camille stayed for lunch, and Dad gradually steered the conversation toward our Bible study. I thought that was the underlying reason for his visit, rather than his refusal to squander a hard-earned Delta freebie. I could sense he was concerned and looking for information, but I had no idea what it was about. "Dad, why don't you just join me tomorrow night?"

"Yes, you should come!""Camille agreed.

"Oh, is it open for visitors?"
"Of course!""I said. "You're my father! People bring tourists all the time." This was not totally accurate. There used to be visitors, but as the evenings became more emotionally close, the presence of an outsider made everyone feel uneasy. It was becoming increasingly difficult to find fresh visitors. Regardless, I was determined to show my father that our small group was onto something worthwhile.

Les returned to Idaho the weekend my father attended the Bible study. Something about his presence had grown so inextricably linked to the emotional highs we typically experienced on Saturday nights that it just wasn't the same without him. The evening proceeded as scheduled: music, Bible reading, debate, and prayer, but nothing remarkable. Dad seemed disappointed based on how much I had hyped it up. He only mentioned "the music was nice" afterward. He also considered it unusual that everyone ignored him.

"I can understand the kids your age," he told them. "I guess it's awkward to be around someone's parents as a young adult. But what is the mother's name?"

"Pam?"

"Right." He inhaled and tilted his head, like he had when I was a child. A gesture that is not simply intended to express pleasure. "Is she always so distant?"

I noted her lack of engagement but gave her credit for being focused. "She's just a neat freak," I explained. "I hadn't told her you were coming ahead of time, and I'm sure she was just stressed out and self-conscious, wishing the house had been cleaner for you."

Overall, the evening appeared to ease Dad's concerns about the group. He didn't bring it up again during the trip. Instead, he focused on pushing me to communicate with my mother more often. They spoke once or twice a month, usually to share notes on my life's progress. I admired that they had found a way to remain cordial and connected following their divorce. When I conveyed this to Dad, he refused to accept the credit.

"That's all your mother," he said. "She worked hard to make that happen so it didn't feel like the family was so broken up. I am pleased she did. "You know me"—he shook his head—"stubborn."

This revelation astonished me and made me wonder if I had gotten some things about Mom wrong. So I decided to follow my father's suggestion and try to connect with her more, beginning with an invitation to my twenty-first birthday celebration.

Having grown up feeling socially alone, I relished any opportunity to bring people together and host. Hospitality was a skill I didn't understand I had until I was on my own. I had a Martha Stewart Living subscription and like setting the tone or creating an environment in which people might meet. For my party, which took place in our apartment's courtyard, I leased a long table for the guests, booked catering from a popular local French café, and even had a champagne fountain brought.
Mina was uncharacteristically sloppy and inattentive while helping me string lights. She finally sat down in a folding chair at the rented table, her head in her hands, elbows resting on the white tablecloth.
"I think Harker is bringing his fiancée tonight," she told me.
"Ohhh, that's correct. I heard she was coming to visit. "I am sorry, Mina."
"I'm just praying that God will take away these sensations! Nothing will ever happen, so why can't I just let it go? "He is all I think about."
I didn't want to give her false optimism, but I was a romantic who hated seeing her hurt. "Mina, I don't believe it's insane to assume something could happen between you two. People frequently break off engagements.
She sniffed, swallowed, and laughed briefly. "I guess that's true."
"Come on, let's fill this thing with Champagne!"
An hour later, the bubbles were flowing, the food was ready, and my "dinner party" mix CD was playing. I'd include some Serge Gainsbourg and one or two songs from Abe's band. I considered putting some Dave Matthews, but I did not want to be reminded of Blue Eyes. He hadn't called yet to wish me a happy birthday, and with him two hours ahead, I was beginning to lose hope. I'd been trying to distract myself over the last few years since that Lincoln Center kiss—developing crushes on cute costars, dating a few guys here and there—but when it came to falling in love, I couldn't allow myself because of the unshakeable belief that Blue Eyes was "the one." Not hearing from him was a stark reminder of the truth: we'd both been building new lives, and I wasn't his first call any longer.
The proof of my new life began to pass through the courtyard gates. Camille and several other people I knew from New York who had

also relocated to the coast, a handful of LA soap actors and costars from recent acting assignments, and pals from my previous florist work. The Bible study group included Pam and Ed, Emily, Abe, and Harker (who was not accompanied by his fiancée). This was the first time I had brought together my Bible study and non-Bible study buddies. They all appeared to be getting along and socializing well, but having them all in one location made it easier to notice the divide between the two groups I had started to develop. I could tell how much more connected, safe, and known I felt with my Bible study group than with anyone else. I could also tell them apart since, other from Camille, none of them drank. I knew they weren't partying, but not even a sip on my twenty-first birthday? So much for the Champagne Fountain.

At the very least, my mother and stepfather appreciated the bubbles. She was pleased to have been invited and was having a good time, circulating through the gathering and smiling and laughing, rather than hanging off to the side or sitting alone at the table. That is, until she began speaking with Pam. I was on the other side of the courtyard, but as their conversation progressed, I noticed Mom's grin fade and her eyes tighten into distrust and mistrust.

I made my way through the crowd to neutralize any anger. As I walked, I passed by my stepfather, who was talking with Harker.

"I hear you are engaged!"My stepfather said." Congratulations, young man!"

"Ah... actually, that is not... currently... We decided to go our separate ways."

What? Had Mina heard anything yet? I would have hurried to locate her, but she would have to wait. My top priority was to get to my mother and Pam.

When I eventually got there, the expression on my mother's face told me she was "tolerating" whatever Pam was saying to her. I arrived just in time to hear Pam's final thinking.

"As parents, we can become so focused on our own issues that we neglect our children's emotional needs." She smiled and petted my hair. "Hello, sweetheart." We were just discussing how very resilient you are, given how much your parents endured.

Whatever my mother is not, one thing is certain: she is extremely intelligent. Her lips moved into a nice closed smile. Then I noticed the blink that she always gives before inhaling and saying something brilliantly/devastatingly cutting. She opened her mouth.

"Wow, diving right in, huh?"I joined in, attempting to lighten the mood.

"She's so impressive," Pam told Mom. "So independent and so young! I wouldn't have been as bold when I was her age. You must be quite proud!"

Les had lately discussed independence with me, and he particularly stated that mine had resulted in an inward revolt against God. "You probably felt neglected as a child, so I can see why you're always trying to control things rather than letting God take care of you," he commented, and Pam concurred. It was a harsh message, but so much of it seemed right, and I didn't want to be too proud to take excellent advise.

Listening to Pam now, I realized her reply to my mother had multiple dimensions. Mom understood it as well, judging by the expression on her face.

Mom reached over and drew me closer to herself in an unexpected display of willpower. Pam's hand dropped off my back.

"Oh, I'm sooooo proud of my little girl," exclaimed her mom. "No, not small girl. You're officially twenty-one!"She furrowed her nose and squeezed me too hard, really laying it on for Pam. "I've got your present. Are you ready?"

"Do I need to be ready?"

"Well, it's something all your friends will enjoy."

That terrified me. "Okayyy."

She found a fork and tapped it on her champagne glass, forcing everyone to quiet down. "All right, everyone," she said. "I've got a special surprise for Joy!"

The courtyard became utterly silent. Mom turned to face me.

"I'm so proud of you," she stated. "You've worked so hard to come to Hollywood, and I know great things are in store for you. It took a long time, but I was finally able to collect all of your wonderful memories in one spot.

She gave me a big scrapbook with a pink ribbon around it. "Ta-da!"

I eagerly slid the ribbon off and unwrapped it. My mother understood how much I enjoyed scrapbooks since my days at Grandma Doris'. It started out strong. Baby photographs with a Crayola ocean and paper palm trees stuck to the page looked back at me. Childhood photographs of me singing were cut and pasted to a flat cardboard stage. But then I turned the page and found myself at the age of five, standing naked in the bathtub. I drew a short breath, embarrassed. I'm meant to share this with my pals to show them my exact shape. It became worse. A playbill featuring images of me from To Kill a Mockingbird and Gypsy was followed by a page torn from my seventh-grade diary, which she had allegedly discovered and read. I had quietly journaled about my first kiss, and now it was in a scrapbook, covered with paper hearts.

I was infuriated. I felt humiliated. I was outraged. I remembered what Les had said at Bible study one Saturday: "If someone wants to label you against the loving truth of who you are, you have the authority to say, 'I don't accept that.' It doesn't matter who they are— a stranger, a parent—don't accept it!"Here you go, Joy." What better time to take this stance? All you need to do is say it. "I don't receive that." Just say it!

But I could not. Not with everyone's "aww"s. I had no choice but to showcase these private moments for the entire audience to view. My mother's expression was filled with happiness and anxious anticipation of my appreciation for all of her hard work. I smiled, hugged her, and exclaimed, "Thank you!" as I reminded myself that this was an audition for the role of appreciative daughter."Loud enough for everyone to hear.

As half of the party looked through the scrapbook, I felt Pam's touch on my back and recognized the familiar floral lingerie-drawer aroma. She peered at me and asked quietly, "Are you okay?""

Tears welled up, but I pushed them down. Not tonight. Not now. I nodded, and she realized I didn't want to talk about it. She grinned and handed me a small gift bag, her shoulders moving up to her ears.

"It's just a little sumthin' to remind you to live in the truth of who you are," she finished. "A patient Beauty, not striving, but resting and waiting for the King."

I laughed. I knew exactly what would be in that bag.

Disney had recently included a "Princess Personality Quiz" in the additional features of one of their remastered DVDs. Pam had discovered this, and, tying it in with Les's words about me being "God's little princess" a few weeks prior, she thought it would be a fun way for all of us "precious daughters" to engage with the idea of our true identity as "daughters of the king," so I joined the group of young women and took this ridiculous quiz. For years, my biggest theatre fantasy was to portray Belle in the Broadway musical Beauty and the Beast. I knew every note from the day that blasted cartoon came out, and I auditioned for the Broadway musical multiple times while still living in New York, often making it to the private producer sessions only to learn Toni Braxton or Debbie Gibson would be playing the role. Nonetheless, I knew my day to play Belle was approaching, so I should have known it was a ruse when this DVD quiz told me I was Sleeping Beauty. Aurora had a terrible, difficult-to-pronounce name, and she did nothing but spin around the woods and stick a big needle into her finger throughout the film. You only had one job, Aurora.

I reached into Pam's purse, and I was correct. Under the tissue paper, there was an enamel Sleeping Beauty key chain. Pam must have informed everyone because after the party, when I opened the rest of my gifts, I discovered a variety of Aurora birthday cards penned with notes about "entering into a season of rest." I also received a NAP QUEEN sweatshirt, a pink mug with nighttime tea, and a sleep mask purchased at Disneyland. Despite how corny it all was, this collection of silly Disney trinkets made me feel more noticed than my own mother's overflowing scrapbook.

Mina and I cleaned up after everyone had departed. I recommended we leave it until the morning, but she was so excited by the news of Harker's broken engagement that she needed something to burn off the energy. We concluded just after midnight. I checked my phone one final time. Nope. He missed it. My twenty-first birthday passed without Blue Eyes' presence. I was gutted. I desired Mina's tenacity and patience. Despite her adversity, she maintained an optimistic attitude. "I know this is just a season," she'd add. "God is about to do something great. I just need to believe Him."

I didn't even know what "trusting God" looked like. God appeared more like a buddy who simply walked alongside me through the mud. At least I wasn't alone, although it wasn't really a rescue. I was still struggling with the same fears, fending for myself as Les and Pam had suggested, and I still felt more like a trash panda than princess. I was becoming restless. Where was the wonderful, wondrous God we worshiped? I needed proof that He was still capable of performing extraordinary and surprising feats.

Then, a few weeks after my birthday celebration, I returned home one night to see candles lighted throughout the apartment. A vase of lovely flowers was on the coffee table in front of Mina, who was cuddled up on the couch and glowing.
"What's up?""I said.
"Harker was just here," she explained. "Joy... he proposed."

CHAPTER SEVEN

Les married Mina and Harker six weeks later, in the woods backyard of the Van Hewitts' large house in Idaho, where Les, Martine, and their sons had settled. There had been no forethought. They decided on a Sunday and got married seven days later. During the ceremony, Les placed the rings in his palm between them, and someone snapped it; a rainbow appeared to float above them. It was an indication from Heaven that God was blessing them. Bless us. God was doing something radical, sacred, and beyond our understanding.
At least that's how Mina described it to me later, when she returned from her wedding to clean up her side of the flat. I hadn't actually received an invitation to the wedding. None of us in LA had been, except Emily, who had grown up with Harker. Les described this as "an intimate, holy event" that only a few people could be trusted to attend. Mina's parents received just a limited invitation due to their reservations about the wedding's timing and age difference. They barely made the cut because Harker believed her parents deserved to be acknowledged and treated with grace. Pam, on the other hand, went dress shopping with Mina and organized a little wedding shower for her, whereas Les provided premarital counseling and planned the rehearsal dinner. Everything was paid for by Ed, the only one with a consistent income.
I was hurt that I was not included. It confirmed that I was still on the outside. The only justification I could think of was my continuous love to Blue Eyes, which indicated that something was still taking the place of God in my heart. He called the day after my birthday to apologize. He had been preoccupied with studying for a major law school exam and had entirely forgotten. His apologies seemed sincere, but we were falling back into our old habits. This was what Les meant when he said I was constantly trying to control things

rather than allowing God to take care of me. This had to be what was preventing me from progressing spiritually. If I'm going to see God do great things in my life, I need to show how dedicated I am. I need to be braver than I've ever been.

So, one afternoon in my now-half-empty apartment, I made the call. When he answered, he could hear voices behind him laughing. "Hey, I didn't take your Civil Procedures book. I finished my brief about a week ago.

"I'm sorry; is this a bad time?"I asked.

"No, J. These idiots are simply leaving. "Hang on." The cacophony subsided, and I could hear him closer now. He sounded like he was sleeping on his bed, the covers muffled the echoes. I could smell him.

"So, actually there's something I wanted to, um..." My breathing was quick and my heart was hammering. "What are we doing?""

"What are we doing?""

"Like, we've been friends for so long, then we've been more than friends, then back to just friends, and..." I didn't know how to get there. I could hear his breathing changing. He did not want to have this conversation. I did not want to have this conversation. What are you doing now? Why are you doing this? Say, "Nevermind," Joy. "Never mind" ! But I was resolute. God was calling me to a wild faith, and there was no room for doubt or, as Les put it, living in second place. I was prepared to toss away anything that might get in my way.

"If we're not going to get married, then I don't know what we're doing."

He did not say anything for a long time. I also lay down on my bed. We were side by side in my head.

"Married? Joy, I'm still in school. I'm not ready to marry someone." The word lingered in his mouth as if he'd never said it before.

"I don't mean right now," I said. "I am not asking you to say you want to be married right now. But I want to know whether that's where you see us going. Joy exclaimed, "I'm just... " "I am in love with you. I have been in love with you for eight years. I can't keep doing this. It is horrible for me. "It hurts me."

He breathed forever. I continued on.

"If you can't tell me that you're at least thinking this is a possibility that we should explore, then I... I have to let you go."

He was calm. Say something. Fight for me. Love me! Say something!

He eventually did. "I'm not sure what to say. I'm just not in a position to make that decision right now.

For the next week, I was unhappy. The melancholy and lethargy were the worst I'd ever encountered. Every day was the same: I read my Bible, slept, wrote in my journal, slept, ate if I felt like passing out, had an infrequent shower while screaming, read my Bible, and slept. Pam came to check on me after I missed the Saturday night meeting.

"I'm so proud of you, Joie," she replied after I detailed what had occurred. "You have let go of the idol you had placed in the place of God." I am very inspired by your faith."

When she saw her words weren't helping, she advised I visit Idaho for a time.

"It's becoming like a little God spa up there," she told me. "I believe it would be beneficial for you to be a child in a family-oriented home. Would you like that?"

I'd enjoy that. That's all I needed. I needed to be surrounded by my family.

Pam left the flat, so I purchased a ticket for the next day. I'd been filming pilots, movies, and TV episodes since I was a preteen, so I was used to boarding planes, arriving at odd airports, and being driven to random locales to meet a group of strangers. So nothing about this made me worried; it was just another excursion to a different location.

As Pam mentioned, their large house in Idaho has become a shelter for many people in need of a tranquil escape. Emily's best friend from college was temporarily staying in a guest room there, and she had been assigned to fetch me up at the airport. Jasmine was short, with a tiny smile between beautiful bubble cheeks, and violet contacts covering her brown eyes.

"Welcome to God Spa!"" she replied, echoing Pam's words as she met me at the terminal. She hugged me. The hugging appeared to extend across state lines. "I'm Jasmine."

"I am Joy. Thank you for making the trip to the airport." I swallowed down a cough that had been building for a few days.

"Easy. I'm happy to help. Oh, sorry! "Let me move those to the back." Her groomed hands grabbed for a little stack of books on the passenger seat. I picked up the last one and gave it to her: French 3.

"Tu parles français!" I exclaimed, pleased to see another Francophile like myself.

"Oui! I return to my level. Are you fluent?"Yes, I am brushing up. Are you fluent?

"I understand more than I say." I laughed. "I visited Paris a couple years ago after graduation, but I haven't practiced since then."

"I'll get over there someday."

Before long, we were exchanging life tales. Jasmine had climbed out of a Las Vegas trailer park, leaving behind two vaguely indifferent parents and a roaming older brother, contrary to my expectations based on her studiousness. She finished summa cum laude with a BS in philosophy and a minor in literature. But, while she had distanced herself from her family, she had not completely avoided disorder. One night, she responded to a crisis call from her lover.

"He'd been acting weird," she explained. "I found him in a parking lot with a stash of crystal meth." Two days later, she arrived at the emergency room with a broken jaw, significant bruising around her neck and wrists, and a rape kit. Emily heard the Van Hewitts had a large house, so she contacted to ask whether her old college buddy Jasmine could spend the summer there. Explore the field behind it. Simply relax and heal. "They wanted to help, but Les and his family were settling in. And then Les said he was glad to have me remain since he wanted to make it a ministry home anyway."

"Oh, he does?""

"Yeah, I believe pastors are often provided a place to reside by the church they work for. But he doesn't want it to just be his place—he's got a vision for a ministry home and a new church. I'm not sure about the details or timeframe, but it's already been a big benefit to me.

Les told Jasmine she could remain as long as she wanted until she was ready for the next phase, whatever it may be. She'd been there for six months at that point.

I gazed outside the window. I had always associated Idaho with potatoes, but this was clearly in a different area of the state. The trees we were driving through at 75 mph already made me feel like I was in a fairytale. The jungle stretched higher than I had ever seen. There was abundant foliage in New Jersey, but the trees did not tower and loom like these evergreens.

"I've never been to the Pacific Northwest," I said.
Jasmine took a deep breath and said, "Oh, I love it here." "It's so quiet."
The sun was shining, so it appeared warm outdoors, yet rain fell on the windshield, and I wrapped my sweater around myself to stay warm. I coughed again.
Jasmine offered me a bottle of water. "I drank out of it already, if that's okay."
"I don't want to get you sick with whatever this cough is," I told you.
"Just have the rest," she replied.
We traveled for miles and miles on the highway until there was a break in the wall of green, a small village appeared, and the Beauty and the Beast music played in my mind. The village is small and quiet.
The wonderful moment did not last long. The farther we drove into town, the less lovely everything got. Mina and Pam had described this location as an ideal refuge, yet among the fast-food joints, strip malls, and chain stores, the only thing not bordered with concrete was a modest brick-faced restaurant named the Bistro, on a corner near abandoned railroad tracks.
After a few more twists and turns, we slowed down on a dirt road lined with midcentury homes. It was the type of country path where kids' bikes sat on overgrown front lawns, and you couldn't tell if they had been there for an afternoon or a year. Jasmine slowed her car and rolled her eyes.
"The gravel road is the worst. If you're not traveling five miles per hour, the rocks will kick up and harm your paint."
The road terminated at what appeared to be a ten-acre field, and we arrived at the Van Hewitts' house, the last one on the left. Perhaps this was the Van Hewitts'. It was now Les's.
It was an unexpected addition to this street of modest homes. White-painted bricks rise brazenly from the earth. The driveway is horseshoe-shaped and paved with brown stones. Bushes were set exactly five feet apart on either side of the path, with small silver lights poised, ready for dusk. From a distance, the home was instantly magnificent and resembled something I had seen previously. What was it? It wasn't just the abundance of information that felt familiar. There was something else, too. The sky was enormous over this stretch of land. All of the trees had been cleared,

leaving the house looking like a dramatic set piece. It did not belong here.

"Ed built this house, you know," Jasmine explained as we turned onto the gravel path. "I guess he modeled it after George Washington's house in Mount Vernon."

That was it. Memories of my ninth-grade field trip to Washington, D.C. came flooding back. Blue Eyes slept next to me in the back of the bus, using headphones. My head is on his shoulder. No, I reminded myself, yanking my focus back to the current moment.

Unlike the first president's immaculately maintained home, the closer we went to the Big House, the more I saw its deterioration. It wasn't in disarray, but knowing Pam's attention to detail, I anticipated the house to be spotless. Instead, wear and tear showed through. The house's white paint had a thin film of filth. Everything was grimy, especially the cars parked out front.

These were what my stepfather referred to as "A to B cars"—unimpressive, but they got you to your destination. An ancient black Camry with bumper damage and an old Mitsubishi Delica that really needed a wash. Someone had scribbled in the window dirt FOR A GOOD TIME CALL xxx-xxx-xxxx. We both saw it at the same time, and Jasmine scoffed and shook her head.

"That is Dontay. He's always playing around," she said with a cheeky smile. "I promise we love Jesus here."

"Hey, Jesus, now is a good time. I am down!"

"Can you image calling that number and just hearing someone share the Gospel?"

I used my best 900-number voice: "Hey, handsome, I can't wait to tell you about Romans 8:38." Jasmine laughed as we parked the car and went inside.

When she opened the front entrance, a tangled gray cat darted past our feet. Jasmine reached down and scooped it up before it could get too far.

"This is Salome." She held the cat up to me. I attempted to smile. Nobody mentioned the cat. "I call her Salami because the boys are always making sandwiches and petting her so—"

"So she smells like salami," I explained for her.

Jasmine chuckled and shut the front door behind us.

I was smacked with that nasty sickly-sweet odor I recalled from meeting Les while he was cooking at the Van Hewitts. Inside, the house was elegantly designed, albeit a few decades old: a marble-floored entryway, pricey linen wallpaper with smudge marks from grimy hands, a rounded cherrywood banister with white-carpeted stairs that were browning in the middle due to foot use. The dining room is to the right, the living room is to the left, and straight ahead is a huge kitchen with a massive bay window. Better Homes & Gardens would have featured this location in 1985.

Les' twins, the Barbarians, sat in the living room and played video games. They did not look at us. We entered the kitchen, where a middle-aged couple sat at a table. The man was playing solitaire. The woman was using soda water to try to get spaghetti sauce off the top of her pink uniform. Jasmine introduced us.

"We have heard so much about you!" the woman said with a southern twang, her platinum hair falling in her eyes as she stood up to hug me." I'm Lucy!"

"Hi, sweetheart. My name is Kurt." Kurt did not move, but the up-and-down glance he gave me felt more intrusive than a hug. He had a bony face and cold blue eyes that darted across my body. I immediately despised him, but then felt horrible for pronouncing judgment on someone I didn't even know.

"Kurt and Lucy are living in the basement," Jasmine stated.

"Temporarily," Lucy added. "We were a part of Les's old church, so we're staying here awhile as we sort out next moves for the new ministry."

"I don't know what you're talking about, I'm just here for the free food," Kurt laughed, and Lucy swatted him playfully.

"Les, Marti, and the boys are upstairs," Jasmine explained. "Pam and Ed live in the garage apartment, and I'll show you where we're staying." She motioned for me to follow.

Jasmine murmured over her shoulder as I followed her down another hallway, "Lucy's the only person I've ever met who sells Mary Kay in real life."

"Is that why she's wearing the old waitress uniform?"

"Yes! Isn't this funny? "She thinks it is glamorous."

"I suppose it is, especially with the blonde hair!"

We went into the only downstairs bedroom.

Windows extend from floor to ceiling. navy velvet curtains. The pearly-striped white linen wallpaper matches the rest of the house. An unmade full-size bed with an empty Cheetos bag and twin bunk beds that were properly tucked in. Jasmine threw her purse onto the top bed.

"You can take the bottom."

I set my suitcase down and looked around. "How many of us are here?""

"Just you, me, and Gretchen."

"Gretchen? I have not met her. And you mentioned Dontay, too? How will I keep track of everyone?"I laughed.

"Ha, I know; it took me a minute, too. Of course, you're familiar with the Van Hewitt family. "Pam, Ed, Harker, and Abe."

"Yes. "And Mina."

"Oh, I wish you had been here for the wedding. "It was amazing."

"That's what I hear," I said, attempting to be pleasant.

She proceeded. "And now you recognize me, Jasmine. Hi! "I'll be the tiny brunette who helps you remember your French."

I smiled. She was entertaining.

"And you just met Kurt and Lucy."

"Skeleton-looking guy and Mary Kay lady."

"He does resemble a skeleton. I'm pleased it isn't only me. They have a thirteen-year-old son. Brandon."

I took a breath. "Brandon. Thirteen. "Son of Skeleton Kurt and Pink Lady Lucy."

"That one won't be hard because there's only four teenagers, Brandon plus Les and Marti's boys."

"Oh, sure," I replied. "Quiet Boy and the Barbarians. That is what I have nicknamed them."

Jasmine laughed. "He's so peaceful, and those twins are crazy! I'll name them that too, just between us."

My gaze moved to the unmade bed. "And Cheetos?" What did you say her name was?"

"Gretchen. She arrived some months after me. She lacks a clear direction. It's not intended to be a judgment. I've always been a driven person, so connecting with her is a problem for me. Her family has comparable problems to mine—addictions, extreme poverty—I suppose it simply affected us differently. But she has a kind heart. Pam met her in Los Angeles last year and employed her as an accounting assistant for Ed's firm.

"Is Gretchen from LA? I'm amazed she didn't attend Bible study.

"I think she moved up here, like, right before you and Camille started

going."
"So you met Camille? I didn't suppose she had been here yet."
"No, I've just heard about the 'gorgeous, redheaded British actress' that Les keeps ribbing Dontay about meeting one day."
I felt it was interesting that Jasmine knew when Camille and I started going to Bible study. What more does she know about us? When I told her my story in the car, she sometimes responded as if she already knew. I hadn't given it much attention at the time because I was so taken with the beauty of the passing trees. But why would Les or Pam share what we discussed in LA with the group here in Idaho? The chats at Bible study were supposed to be private. I told myself that showed they cared about all of us and looked forward to bringing everyone together. I felt confident that neither of them would reveal anything about me with anyone unless they were trustworthy.
Les and Pam had not given us much information on the Idaho group, so Jasmine told that Dontay played college football on scholarship and was anticipated to be drafted, but he tore his ACL. He was so depressed following his injuries that he dropped out of school and went hiking in the Pacific Northwest. Then one weekend, he arrived at Les' old church.
"Les has been mentoring him ever since," Jasmine explained. "He came along with Les and Marti when they moved here."
"His family doesn't mind that he recently moved in with another household?"
"Single mother. Dontay says she's glad he's experiencing a familial environment that she couldn't offer. "Les calls him his 'adopted son.'"
"Aww. Okay. Dontay. Football. Call him and have a fantastic time. "I get it."
"Haha. Exactly. And that includes everyone in the home! You'll meet a few more individuals on Wednesday night, but don't worry about it right now.
I had heard about the Wednesday night Bible study from several of the LA guys who had come before me. It sounded similar to our Saturday night group, but strangely more profound. No one could ever pinpoint exactly what the "magic" was, but there was a reason this large house was affectionately referred to as "God Spa". Every time someone returned from a visit here, they claimed incredible personal improvement and appeared even more committed to their

beliefs. People here definitely took life and faith seriously.

"So," I asked, "what do we do now?""

"That's kind of the great thing about being here," Jasmine added. "Everyone will give you the freedom to do anything you need to. You can go exploring. There's a lovely walk through the field in the back. You can journal while lying in bed, play the piano, or hang out at the kitchen table. Simply make time to connect with the Lord in whichever way you need. There is no anticipation. "Just be.

No expectations. It seemed inconceivable. There were always expectations. To prepare, perform, deliver, speak up, remain silent, relax, behave, and be intelligent. There were expectations to pay attention, arrive on time, be professional, be unique but not crazy, and be creative without making others uncomfortable. Be collaborative, yet believe your intuition. Be tough. Be sweet. Smile. Sing it out, Louise! My life had been like one of my father's adventure courses: balancing and avoiding. What would it be like to just be myself?

My phone chimed. Mom texted about wanting to come out to Los Angeles for lunch that weekend. I hadn't told her or Dad that I was going to Idaho since I was seeking for more ways to assert my independence from them. The more I immersed myself in Les and Pam's world, the more I felt misunderstood by my parents and lost trust in them.

I ignored her message and followed Jasmine's first suggestion: a solo walk in the field behind the Big House. As a general rule, I was more comfortable alone than with others, owing to the expectations that typically accompanied company. I knew it was strange to turn up as a guest in someone's home and then leave to roam over their lush acres on my own, but it was what I wanted. That was completely me in that time. I figured what better way to practice being completely myself than with a group of virtual strangers?

So I wandered. I daydreamed. I opened the journal I'd brought along and composed a song, then selected flowers and made a bouquet before returning home just as dinner was completed cooking. Les and Marti were delighted to see me. Pam and Ed, too. They were in town that weekend. It was a full house, and the laughing and loud voices during the meal were a welcome change after spending the previous week alone in my apartment. Dontay was the loudest and most noisy of the group. He was twenty-one, but he still acted like a teenager. He arrived for supper fresh from his shift at the Mobil station, dressed in coveralls that fit snugly over his huge football player figure. He never stopped speaking, fidgeting, or moving. He was pure comedy. He even got a smile from Quiet Boy, who I'd observed gazing at me a couple of times before running away. It was not the same as Kurt's leering expression. Much more innocent. He wasn't my type—no chance—but after Blue Eyes' rejection, I was glad to get the confidence boost.

I disliked going to bed right after eating, but my cough was growing worse, so I decided it was best to get some rest. Among the chatter and bustle as plates were cleaned, someone gave me a red glass bottle of cough medication. I had a teaspoon, then went to my room, changed into my pajamas, and slid into the bottom bunk with my journal. As I laid there reflecting on the day, one thing occurred to me: unlike at the Van Hewitt house, Les was not wearing shoes inside.

CHAPTER EIGHT

My face hurt. My mouth was stale. Why did I feel so tired? I moved my head and felt the flannel pillowcase tear from my face, where crusted saliva had tied us together. The corner of a book was under my pillow at the perfect angle to cause a painful dent in my jaw. My journal. I was in a dark room with big windows covered in blackout curtains. I heard voices outside, and the sound guided me. The door was behind my head.
Right. I'm in Idaho.
I forced myself up and took long breaths, blood flowing back into my limbs. As my feet landed on the dirty carpet, my Coldplay Parachutes t-shirt and red French-cut underwear untucked. A crack of light emerged from beneath one of the curtains. I stumbled over whatever wrappers or debris were on the floor beside Gretchen's bed and pulled back the big blue curtain.
The light filled the room, and I placed my face against the cold glass. Heat emitted from the floor vent. Why is the heat turned on in the summer? I fumbled with the window lock. A nice breeze blew in, and my mind began to clear. I have never had to pee more in my life. I discovered my sweatpants in a bundle at the foot of the bed I'd been

sleeping in, grabbed my glasses, and went to the nearest restroom, which was in the kitchen.

Someone exclaimed, "She lives!" I hadn't put on my glasses yet, so it was difficult to see who was in the room. I smiled through cracked lips and lifted my hand to say hello.

"You really are a sleeping beauty." I recognized Pam's voice.

"I guess so!" I replied. I locked the bathroom door behind me and peed for a whole minute. I cupped some water in my mouth, splashed my face, put on my glasses, and returned to the kitchen.

Just like the night before, the room was alive with joyous chatter, a sound I had coveted in my quiet and tight childhood homes. Martine was washing the dishes. Kurt and Lucy were in the same chairs. Pam was playing checkers at the kitchen table with Gretchen, who had started eating a new bag of Cheetos.

Jasmine was painting her toenails on the floor in the corner next to the table. She grinned up at me. I looked at the microwave clock, which read 4:07 p.m. Wow, I slept for nearly 24 hours.

"Every time I went in the room yesterday, you were out," Jasmine told me.

"What do you mean 'yesterday'?" I said." "What day is it?"

"Monday."

"Monday?" I inquired, still rubbing sleep from my eyes. "What, did I sleep for two days?"

"Almost!" she said. "I guess you needed the rest."

It seemed to have eased my cough, which had subsided.

The Barbarians continued to play video games on the living room couch, this time with Kurt and Lucy's son Brandon. Someone was poorly playing the same four bars of a song on the piano. I craned my neck to see Quiet Boy bent over the keys and wished to hear the strum of Abe's guitar instead.

Kurt was discussing The Matrix, which he had recently seen for the first time: "I enjoyed the 'unplugging' connection to actual life as being more than what we can perceive. I felt as if God was urging me to question the world's illusions and distractions and recognize the underlying truth."

Oh, did you notice that? What is the overall message of the film?

Why was I so snarky? This is not LA, Joy. Most people do not study cinema for a living. Stop being so judgmental. I was tired. And hungry.

"It's like that Pierre Chardin quote," Jasmine replied, concentrating on applying the dark purple shellac perfectly. "We are not human beings going through a spiritual experience. "We are spiritual beings having a human experience.

Everyone stared at her, puzzled.

"Allow me to translate," Jasmine added, giggling. "We are not humans having a spiritual experience. "We are spiritual beings having human experiences."

"Who is Pierre Shar-don?" Lucy murmured to Pam in a southern insult to French. Pam shrugged.

"Oh, you're so fancy," Kurt replied with an edge in his voice. He was smiling, but in the way a mad child does before skinning a cat.

The front door banged open.

"Boys," Les said, "come help with the groceries!" The piano abruptly stopped, and Quiet Boy walked through the kitchen and out the front door. The barbarians hopped to.

Realizing I hadn't checked my phone in two days, I took it from the bedroom, where I had plugged it in before going to bed.

Twenty-six missed calls. Mom was 19, Dad was 5, and Camille was 2. What in the world? I called Mom back first, returning to the kitchen with the phone in my ear.

"Oh, thank God!" she said.

"Is everything okay?" I asked.

"Where are you, Joy?" We've been worried sick! Your father and I have been trying to find you.

"Why, what happened?"

"What happened?" "You disappeared!"

"I did not disappear. I traveled to Idaho to visit my buddies. What do you mean, you've been looking for me? "I have only been away from my phone for two days."

"When you didn't respond to my texts and calls since Friday, I became concerned. "I'm not sure where you are, where these people live, or if you're okay."

I remembered what Les and Pam had told us about setting boundaries with those in our lives who try to keep us believing the same lies about our identity. I was not going to let my mother's struggles with control make me feel compelled.

"Mom," I continued, "I am an adult." If I want to jump on a plane and go visit some pals, I can do it without telling you."

As everyone became aware of what was going on, the kitchen became quieter.
I know you can, Joy. But if someone is worried about you and keeps calling and texting you, it's just nice to let them know you're fine."
"But, Mom, why is it my obligation to make you feel better when you're acting unreasonable? "Just because you want something doesn't mean I have to give it to you."
"Joy, we don't know these people!" She increased her voice before lowering it again. "It's okay for parents to be concerned about their child if they don't hear from her in days."
"But I'm not a child."
Les and Quiet Boy made a noisy entrance via the front door. QB was laughing at Les as he was delivering a story. "...my God, the waitress's eyes went as big as your mother's nipples when you boys were still suckin' on 'em!"
Pam fluttered her hand to silence them. I entered the hallway.
"I didn't say you were," Mom responded. "I mentioned you were our child. Honey, you will always be my daughter, no matter how old you get. And I believe it is the ethical thing to do to let someone who is concerned about you know that you are fine. You only had to send a text. Your father even called Camille, who reported you did not react to her either!"
"What? "Why does he have Camille's number?"
"I do not know. I guess she picked him up from the airport once, and he wanted to be able to contact you if he needed to, because you never call back!"
I was finished. "Okay, Mom. I'm not sure what you want me to say. I am fine. I'm in Idaho for a couple of weeks. Everything is fine. You don't have to worry."
She sighed and paused. "When are you coming back?"
"I don't know, after the Fourth of July."
"Okay. Will you kindly react when I text you?"
"I'll respond when it feels appropriate."
"What does that mean?"
"We are about to eat dinner, Mom. I'll have to talk with you later."
She exhaled again. "Okay. Please call your father and tell him you're fine."
I hung up. Everyone in the kitchen was talking again, allowing me some privacy. Pam emerged in the corridor and wrapped her arms

around me. I started crying.

"Oh, there now." She petted my head. "I am proud of you. It's difficult to create boundaries. Yes, ma'am, growing can be painful at times."

I nodded and wiped my eyes. Pam gave me a little, folded tissue. She always had a small plastic envelope of tissues in her purse or pocket, just in case somebody started sobbing—because crying signaled growing. In addition to embraces, we were strongly encouraged to cry.

I texted my father as she wrapped an arm around me.

Hey, I am fine. I just got sick and took some cough medicine, which knocked me out. Love you.

I returned to the kitchen to make more pedantic observations on Neo and Morpheus.

"I'm gonna go take a shower and get ready for dinner," I joked. I returned to the guest room to get my toiletries and a towel. The girls in the guest room were requested to shower in the basement, which was Kurt and Lucy's bathroom. The upstairs shower was for Les' boys, and we were advised that "it wouldn't be appropriate." I would have preferred to use Ed and Pam's shower in the garage apartment because I knew them better, and being naked in a stranger's bathroom felt uncomfortable. But I was a visitor, so I didn't want to be fussy.

As I was leaving the bedroom, I noticed the large red bottle of medicine I had taken resting on the dresser. It appeared larger than I remembered—too enormous for an over-the-counter cough suppressant. This was prescribed medication. The label was worn, and the expiration date was a few years old. I turned it over in my fingers, the milky syrup covering the inside of the half-empty bottle. I read the label.

KURT B—
HYDROCODONE

Strange, I thought. It's strange that someone would simply pass over an expired vial of codeine. Didn't I just take a spoonful? Why had it knocked me out for so long?

I carried the bottle out and returned it to Kurt in the kitchen. "Here's your medication back. "That stuff is strong!"

Lucy paused mid-sentence and gazed at the bottle. "What is that?"

"That medicine I took for my cough."

Kurt took it from me before Lucy could study it. "Thank you for bringing it back. I am delighted it helped."

Lucy appeared disturbed. She looked at Les, who had been unbagging groceries but had suddenly stopped and was staring at Kurt. Lucy stared back at me. "How much of this did you take?"

I felt in peril but couldn't figure out why. "Umm, I don't remember taking more than a spoonful."

"Well, you must've taken more than that to sleep for 36 hours," she remarked in a critical, even accusatory tone, yet her eyes began to well up.

I looked between her and Kurt, who was staring at the floor, as if he were the one in peril. I did not comprehend.

"Well, we're glad you're back to life!" Les called out. "This is gonna be a fun couple of weeks!"

CHAPTER NINE

Later, those two weeks in Idaho would serve as a watershed moment for me. Would I have avoided everything if I had stayed in Los Angeles, miserable and mopey over Blue Eyes? Possibly. But then I would not have had Rosie. I think about that every time I share my story. It was all worth it to her.

My first few days at the house were spent exactly like my first afternoon: roaming the neighboring acres, creating songs, and birdwatching. However, I quickly became tired of being alone and began spending more time with the group. We played softball on a nearby field. Despite my poor team sports skills and inability to knock a ball into fair zone, everyone encouraged and cheered me on. We cooked together, helping Les make his meat-heavy feasts while also contributing our own specialties. For the Fourth of July, I cooked strawberry shortcake cupcakes and printed small Declaration of Independence papers to serve them with. I even scorched the edges to make the paper appear older, and it was lovely to be recognized for my hospitality talents. I cut flowers from the garden and arrange them in bouquets to place on the kitchen table or in the restrooms. I also joined Jasmine and Marti in their long-overdue effort to vacuum and thoroughly deodorize the house. The building was an indoor playground for Les's lads, and it began to smell like a locker room.

We mostly talked, though. Raw, sensitive conversations erupted at any moment, whether in the kitchen, the living room, Ed and Pam's garage apartment, on the front porch, or during the odd supper in town at the Bistro (or whatever chain restaurant the crew was in the mood for).

Wednesday nights were when the deepest chats took place. I had heard that these meetings would be more rigorous than regular Saturday Bible studies, but I had no idea how much more.

"The Jezebel spirit is attacking this body of believers," Les told the congregation assembled in the living room on the Wednesday following the Fourth. He sat on the redbrick hearth, holding aloft a stack of thin, fold-over pamphlets to circulate around the room. Everybody took one. Emily had come to visit and was living on the sleeper couch in Ed and Pam's garage apartment, despite the fact that her father still lived in her old home just a short drive away. There was also a young couple named Juana and Miguel, whom I had just met that night. They met the gang through Juana's job at a bank. Pam had gone in to do some banking a few months earlier, and when she and Juana started talking, the subject of religion came up—as it always did among group members—and Pam invited her and Miguel to the Wednesday night meetings.

"Manipulation is happening all around us," Les continued. "In culture, our homes, and Hollywood, where many of our California Family members minister. Pressing into friendship and community is how we grow and hold each other in check when there are so many distractions from the Lord. "The enemy despises relationship." "Relationship" was Les' new buzzword preoccupation. "The more we thrive, the more attacks the enemy will launch against us. Outside resistance is proof that we're on the right track.

The stack came to me. Revealing Jezebel: Manipulation, Seduction, and Rebellion against Authority. I took one and passed the others around.

"In case you aren't familiar with the narrative, Queen Jezebel was the worst example of deception and control in the Bible, and King Ahab was her husband who delegated his authority to her. She walked all over him, worshipped Baal's idols, and murdered hundreds of God's prophets, while Ahab stood by because she was so alluring. "Just like the snake in the garden."

This was new to me. They did not discuss Ahab and Jezebel in Sunday school. My father never taught me about Old Testament characters that are still active in the world today as oppressive spiritual entities that I must remain vigilant about. Listening to Les talk made me feel so naive. I was a sponge.

"Eve preferred to do things her own way in the garden. She did not want God to be in control; she wanted to be in control, therefore she rebelled. Now, what is the first thing this spirit does? "Creates doubt." Les held up his thumb. "We have to guard our hearts against anything and anyone that makes us doubt what we already know is true." He extended his index finger. "The second thing it does is control and create rebellion."

"Uh, technically that's two things, Pop," Dontay said, smiling. A few chuckles lightened the mood in the room.

Oh, he calls him. "POP," I thought. As if he was truly adopted. That's quite sweet. I had only known Dontay for a week, but I was already developing feelings for him. His muscles moved and rippled when he sprinted around the baseball bases or simply stooped over to rummage through a pile of bottle rockets. His cheerful smile was infectious. Even after changing out of his coveralls, he still smelled faintly of gasoline. I felt safe with him. Blue Eyes made me realize I was completely screwed up. I wondered if this was what romance was intended to be: a sense of safety, almost familial love. Aside from his generally juvenile antics, which I convinced myself he'd outgrow, I enjoyed his company. Especially how he appeared to be able to make fun of Les in a manner that no one else could. Well—usually.

Les wasn't laughing or smiling now. He just stared at Dontay blankly. "No. It is the same thing, because revolt seeks independent control. The easiest approach to avoid the seduction of being self-willed is to pursue a relationship. Trust each other to see our blind spots, and be brutally honest with ourselves when our thoughts lead us astray."

"Doubting what, specifically?" Emily asked.

"Doubting what God has already told us is true."

"So, like, questioning what we already believe?"

Les cocked his head. "Do you believe the truth?"

Emily blinked. "Yes."

"Then it is not a belief." It is true.

I raised my hand, and Les grinned at me. He mimicked a schoolteacher and exclaimed, "Yes, Joy!"

Everyone chuckled as I read the booklet's cover. "What does Rebellion Against Authority mean in this context?"
"Well, who is your spiritual authority, Joy?"
"I mean... God."
Les laughed. "Yes, clearly God. But what about here on Earth? Is there anyone you let have spiritual influence over you?"
It seemed like a trap question. My parents? I thought. Not anymore. The Pope? If I was Catholic! My response was: No. No person has spiritual authority over me. But that seemed like the incorrect answer.
"Could you explain what you mean? For example, I comprehend the concept of authority. We have a boss at work who has control over us, and we must follow their instructions. Alternatively, a parent exercises authority over a child. "But, spiritually—"
"The Bible has numerous examples of partnerships in which one person is given spiritual authority over another. Saul and David; Elisha and Elijah; Moses and Jethro. God assigns other people to assist us when we require advice or are making poor decisions due to our own blind spots. So, for example, if you were attempting to control things and someone with spiritual power in your life warned you against it but you disregarded them, it is rebelling against God's authority in your life."
Lucy spoke up: "You're not married, but, if you were, your husband would be your spiritual authority." She massaged Kurt's leg.
My chest tightened suddenly. Despite hearing this phrase my whole life in church, gender roles in American Christianity never felt right to me, my mother, or either of my grandmothers. But, in the context of this Jezebel chat, it dawned to me that perhaps that was just the idea. I came from a long history of assertive, domineering women, so perhaps the Jezebel spirit had already infected my family and my thinking. Maybe that's why I never got on board with the "submissive wife" concept. Was I under attack by an ancient spirit of control? Was being a woman in submission the missing piece—the reason Blue Eyes couldn't see a future with me?
"It's not just a question for single people," Pam added, turning to face Miguel and Juana. "Who is helping to guide you and keep you on the right track?"
"To me, that's you, Pop, and Mama," Dontay told Les and Marti. "You are not my biological family; nevertheless, you are my spiritual

family. "And you, Ed and Pam."
"Oh, yeah, in that case, me too," Jasmine answered. "Kurt, Lucy, and you as well. You are all older than us, with more knowledge and experience. There is a natural order in any Christian community. Pastors, deacons, elders, and so on. Within this community of believers, you three older couples are who I consider to have spiritual authority in my life. I mean, you're like our spiritual parents."
"I agree," Gretchen replied, nodding.
"Definitely," Emily answered.
Juana and Miguel exchanged apprehensive looks. Juana paused for a bit before responding, "Well, I mean, yes, following that logic, I suppose it does make sense."
Quiet Boy, as usual, remained quiet.
Les glanced at me hopefully.
I wish I had asked him one thing then: Who has spiritual power over you? Such a simple and important question to ask any leader, spiritual or not. I did not inquire, however. Instead, I reflected on who had recently made the most significant investment in me. Pam was becoming the warm, loving mother I had never had. Les was becoming the emotionally available father figure that I had always desired. This entire bunch seemed like the boisterous, fun, authentic family I had envisioned. If anyone could assist me figure out the appropriate way to live, it would be them.
"Joy?" Les inquired. "Does that resonate with you?"
"Oh man," I replied with a smile. "Absolutely."

CHAPTER TEN

Mina had moved in with Harker, and I couldn't afford the rent on our house. It was a spacious two-bedroom in Beverly Hills, and I required a longer-term answer. I had gotten the cheerleading role in Bring It On Again, but while I had some funds from previous jobs, I had no idea how long it would be until my next job came in. I discovered an ad for a studio apartment in the Valley. It had a window that viewed additional flats and was on a busy main road, but what drew me in was its proximity to the Van Hewitts. No more languishing in Coldwater Canyon gridlock for 55 minutes, or, God forbid, on the 405. People would soon be driving to me, as my apartment became the group's secondary hub.

That summer, Mina revealed she was pregnant. What she had with Harker was everything I wanted when I got married, which didn't appear to be anytime soon. The dating environment in Los Angeles wasn't for me. I'd been on a few dates, but I always felt utterly inept and bumbling. Dontay was the closest boy I could envision dating since I'd cut out Blue Eyes, and after those two weeks in Idaho, I had a lot of those fantasies. In reality, the distance rendered it impractical.

I was certain that the reason I hadn't met a mate yet was that I hadn't yielded sufficiently for God to reward me. Mina was willing to forego acting, and see how she got rewarded! I didn't feel obligated to give up my acting career, but I realized I needed to make some sort of active sacrifice that would help others. One Saturday night, I informed the group that I would offer up my new apartment to anyone who wanted to pray at any time. I wanted my home to be a haven. Any time of day or night. There's no need to call or check in. The door would always remain unlocked. I had no concern about it and was confident that the Lord would reward my sacrifice by protecting me from those who could rob or assault me.

Emily was the first visitor. One morning at 6:30 a.m., she walked in silently and pressed play on the stereo, which I had prepared with a worship CD. I noticed my small reading light turn on and heard the whoosh and flip of her Bible pages as she hummed along with the music. Lying on the canopy bed I inherited from Mina, I envisioned God in Heaven flipping through His book of single men, picking which one I'd soon crash shopping carts with in a grocery store meet-cute.

Other members would stop over every now and then, once or twice per week. There were just nine of us now, with some attendees dropping off during the year since Les's arrival. We didn't need to communicate during these drop-ins; it was clear that my home was a safe place to rest, and I enjoyed being able to provide something I had spent my whole life seeking.

Then one night at midnight, Camille called me. She was whispering. I could barely hear what she was saying, but the panic in her voice was clear.

"Are you okay?" I inquired.

"Some really intense things have been happening in my apartment lately."

"Like what?" I asked.

"Um... God, this sounds so crazy." She paused. "Can I just come over and stay on your couch tonight?"

"Of course, come over!"

"I just... I think I'm seeing things."

"What are you seeing?"

She took a long breath. "Demons."

Camille had phoned me before, telling me about remarkable events in her life. Every Saturday night, I noticed how well she paid attention and even took notes. She was listening to sermons on tape from various ministers and going to different churches. She took her religion journey very seriously.

It appeared like the more she accepted Jesus into her daily life, the more He showed up for her. She'd have a dream about a high school classmate she hadn't spoken with in years. She resolved to pray and fast for them, and two days later, the individual called her. She'd also been dealing with a lot of stress from her ex-boyfriend, who was suicidal and obsessed with her. She prayed to God for help, and within a week, the man had left town and moved on. I was honestly a little envious of how swiftly and powerfully God was working in her life. What was she sacrificing that I wasn't? More than anything, I was pleased and motivated to see someone's religion grow from rote religious activity to fellowship with God.

"Well, apparently whatever spiritual door I've opened is letting in more than just God," she explained as we sat on my couch. I had prepared some tea before she arrived, but she was too anxious to consume it. "The last several nights, I've woken up completely immobilized in the middle of the night. Tonight I was lying in my bed, unable to move, and this dreadful black—I don't want to be overdramatic, but I don't know what else to call it—demonic figure hovered over me. Basically, they're keeping me down. Then more arrived, and they were crowded around my chamber. And all I could think of was to say 'Jesus,' but it seemed like they were choking me and I couldn't utter anything."

"And you weren't dreaming?"

"No. Absolutely not. "I wish I had been."

"What did you do?"

"I've just prayed. "In my mind." She gave out a surprised laugh. It was the weirdest thing. I just shouted out to Jesus in my head until I could get it out, and then they departed. "Like shrieking."

"Oh, wow, Cam." I shake my head. "Wow."

"Yeah." She looked at me and fiddled with the strings on her sweatshirt. "You don't seem alarmed. Have you ever experienced something supernatural?

I had.

I only had one meeting with God, which I could not describe and never told anyone about. When I was still living in New York City, I left my apartment to go on a "thinking walk" around Union Square, which was my favorite exercise for generating ideas, problem-solving, or practicing lines for an audition. As the mild drizzle grew into a severe rain, I ducked into a little café that was completely deserted, save for the workers. I was greeted by the aroma of bacon and coffee. They let me take the largest booth available, a horseshoe-shaped bench beside a large window. I sat near the edge to watch people through the glass and got a glass of freshly squeezed orange juice.

Life was good. I was 19. My work on Guiding Light was fulfilling for the time being. My church life was full, and my friendships were vibrant. Sitting in the café, casually thinking about Blue Eyes and our strange little merry-go-round, I began to chat to God in my head, as I sometimes did. Then I had a completely new thought.

For a brief period, the rainy city street appeared simple. Sort of boring and genuine. All of the romantic icing I used to apply on everything in my thoughts melted away (don't tempt me, I WILL sing "MacArthur Park"), and I got the following thought: What if all of this Jesus stuff is just nonsense? Made up.

The "Jesus stuff" was working for me, and I was satisfied overall. I figured that worst-case scenario, we'd all convinced ourselves of various things to make life simpler, so I'd keep believing. I figured I'd find out after I die.

Then everything became warm.

My heartbeat slowed. My skin suddenly reached a perfect temperature, as if all of the cells in my body were moving in sync with the sun and my blood was a slow river. Someone sat beside me in my vacant café booth. There was no meat. There is no body to touch. There was only the deep and familiar presence of someone leaning in and speaking softly into my ear. The voice was gentle,

male, joyous, and substantial. Did I feel breath?
"Never doubt that I am real," I was told.
My eyes welled up with tears, and I remained motionless. The voice spoke, then disappeared. I was not paralyzed or shocked; I simply became still in the desperate goal of feeling that presence again. Or to hear the voice again. Even recalling it in my head. But it was simply out of grasp. The only thing that remained was a feeling of pure love wrapping every molecule and cocooning me in an ocean of it, right there where I sat on sticky red vinyl, on a pissy rainy day, in the greatest city in the world. I could have stayed there forever.
"I think supernatural things happen all over the world all the time," I informed you. "Perhaps less so in Western society, because we are so quick to disregard it. Well, we disregard the positive spiritual aspects anyhow. Everyone like ghost stories, but I suppose angels and Jesus are too farfetched. However, many other civilizations incorporate spiritual encounters into their daily lives.
"Well, I really don't know what to do with this," she told me. "I just want to get a nice night's sleep. I do not need dementors in my bedroom!"
I laughed. "On the bright side," I added, "you now know how to make them leave! "Who needs a priest?"
I smiled. She smiled back, but her mood remained unsettled.
"Look, I'm not an expert on this stuff," I said, "but I do believe there is an ongoing fight between good and evil in the globe. Your relationship with God is growing, and it wouldn't surprise me if something spiritually dark tried to scare you away from it. Do you know? Keep you from feeling God's love and becoming more of who you truly are."
Camille nodded her head. "That makes sense."
"Can I pray for you?" I asked.
She nodded again. I held her hand and breathed deeply. I closed my eyes and envisioned the universe's creator shrinking down to human size and sitting in the room next us. I disliked praying openly because it made me feel inadequate. I couldn't quote Scripture like Harker or Les, and I wasn't always sure what to ask for, but as I prayed, I could feel Camille's stress easing away. My prayer brought her comfort, and I could feel it.
In that moment, with my eyes closed, I thought of Les and how difficult it must be for him to always shoulder the weight of others.

People seek for assistance, wisdom, and prayer. The notion made me thankful that I was being led by someone so strong and selfless, because while it felt nice to be a conduit for peace in Camille, I also felt something else, something that, in the wrong hands, could be used to manipulate and abuse: power.

CHAPTER ELEVEN

That Christmas, instead of traveling to either of my parents' houses and, as Les put it, "pressing into" the family I'd inherited through their new marriages, I went to Idaho. Everyone, save Camille, had been invited by Les and Pam to exercise our right to "break away from the expectations other people put on us." I found out later that she had been excluded. I believed she'd chosen to spend Christmas with her family. Looking back, I wish I had seen her exclusion for what it was: Les realized Camille lacked the weaknesses he needed in a victim. Her family was intact, she had a solid foundation of love and support outside of the group, and despite all of her supernatural encounters, she approached faith more rationally than emotionally. Camille was too unpredictable, whereas I was a sure thing.

My parents were upset, as expected. I had been moving back and forth between them on holidays since they split to make things fair for both of them, but it didn't feel right to me. I was tired of extended family gatherings with the new spouses' second cousins, as well as the constant queries about being an actor. I wanted to celebrate Christmas while also feeling like I belonged.

They were hardly the only upset parents. Dontay told me how bewildered and sad his mother was that she had not been invited to spend the holiday with him. The same goes for Emily's father. He still lived in her childhood home, close to the Big House. He couldn't understand why she would return to town and stay there instead of staying with her family, why she would just come over on Christmas Eve, and why he wasn't allowed to visit the Big House on Christmas Day. They had already spent numerous holidays with the Van Hewitts!

Emily just told her father that there was no more room now that Les and his family had moved in and everyone was visiting from out of town. The true reason was what Pam had told all of us: "This is a special time for us with Jesus and each other. We don't want the Holy Spirit's flow to be disrupted by someone who isn't part of the circle of trust and vulnerability we've formed."

Les agreed: "Not everyone belongs in the war room, you know?" We must honor and safeguard God's call on our community."

Neither of us questioned this. It made complete sense to us.

On Christmas Eve, while Emily was at her father's, the rest of us gathered in the living room. Everyone was present, including Juana and Miguel. Piled onto the couches, filling up the floor space, dining room chairs were brought in to ensure that everyone had a place to sit. Seeing the Los Angeles and Idaho groups together in one space seemed significant. We were more than buddies; we belonged together—to each other. I reasoned that this must be how family should feel.

Les has a new book to share. He discovered a Welsh "prophet" who was gaining traction in the charismatic group after writing a book called Designing group Prayer. As before, copies of the book were distributed.

"I feel so much of Heaven's heart in this book, friends," Les exclaimed. Salami got onto his lap and stroked her in his own Godfather-themed show. "The Lord gave me a vision that we were all aboard a ship together. The sea became choppy, and several of us were terrified and wanted to abandon ship, but we all said the same prayer over and over until the waters calmed. Then I saw this book and realized it was meant for us. If we stay in the boat, God will equip us with the tools we need to overcome any obstacle. We need to utilize everything the Lord has revealed to us and design prayers that we may repeat at any time."

"So, this is how crafted prayers work," Pam stated. She had an open notebook on her lap and a pen in her hand. "Abe will play some music on the piano, and you will just scream out anything God brings to mind: the name of a person you want to pray for, a relationship you want restored. I'll write it all down, and then we'll use it to build a prayer that we can all say every day until our prayers are answered."

Harker stood up to turn down the lights and light some candles before sitting back down next to Mina, her lovely big tummy a witness to how much God was blessed her for being an example of a devoted, submissive wife. The atmosphere lightened, and Abe began playing a worship tune. It felt serene and secure. QB took hold of a little djembe, and the sound grew louder. Everyone began singing. I closed my eyes and joined in harmony, my voice rising slightly above the others.

Les read from Matthew as QB banged out a solid pace on the drums. Les had now taken over all of the meetings, and I was curious how Harker and Abe felt about it. It felt natural for Les, a pastor, to host meetings in his own home—except it wasn't. I looked at Harker, wondering what it would be like to have Les move into their childhood home, become best friends with their mother, and take over leadership of the Bible study. Maybe it is a relief. They're too young to be disciplining such a huge group. I chose to see it this way and admired the brothers' humility.

"Let the small children come to me, and do not prevent them, because the kingdom of God belongs to such as these. Truly, I tell you, anyone who does not welcome the kingdom of God as a tiny child will never enter it.' Mmm," remarked Les. "We're over here trying to be independent and accomplish things on our own, but He's given us each other as a physical manifestation of His presence. To encourage and hold each other accountable. You want to see the Kingdom of Heaven? The way is to live surrenderedly, as if we were small children."

I didn't want to be harsh and tough and accomplish everything on my own anymore. Feeling more secure and more ease, I was the first to offer a composed prayer.

"That the Lord would show me how to be innocent and reliant on Him again, like a kid," I exclaimed as the piano and rhythm continued. Ed, bobbing his head as usual, reached over and patted my back. When I gazed at him, he grinned with sweet eyes.

After everyone had said their prayers, the music stopped and we took a little break to allow Pam to go through and organize all of her notes. I fetched some water from the kitchen, and Les caught up with me.

"That was sweet, baby," he murmured. "I am proud of you. I believe that will be extremely significant for you in the next chapter of your life. Relying on God as a child. Relying on the spiritual parents He has placed in your life to represent Him here. You'll notice a lot of mending in the places in your heart where you get to be parented."

"Thank you, Les. I'm delighted to have you take on the job for me," I said.

"You have such a pretty singing voice," Les told you.

"Aw, thank you," I replied.

"But sometimes you overpower everyone and it can be a little distracting."

I instantly felt horrible. Of course, I was in the way. "Sorry... Shoot, I'm sorry."

"I just know honesty is important to you, and we've got to live in a space where we can say uncomfortable things to each other and let it be okay."

"No, I am delighted you told me!" I tried to keep my voice softer, basically mouthing the words. I'd rather know!"

"I figured you would." He smirked and returned to the living room. I felt disappointed in myself, but I was grateful that someone cared enough to tell me the truth and believe in my ability to manage it. In some ways, it reminded me of how much my father valued me—he always felt I was capable. But there was an element of trust between us that had been absent for a long time, and it seemed like Les was filling the void.

Though everyone had requested a variety of prayers, such as Emily's desire to view others and herself the way God saw her, the final created prayer was adjusted to accommodate everyone. Before the end of the visit, we were each handed a small card that Pam had even laminated, on which was typed:

Lord, I am a child in need of help. Teach me to be discriminating and not put my trust in the wrong people. Release me from the obligation to meet others' expectations of me. Familial tendencies no longer define who I am.

It was, of course, a deliberate strategy to separate us from our loved ones. Les found it simpler to manipulate us as we functioned more like a family. He didn't have to be covert about it anymore. One afternoon during that holiday visit, he casually used a term I'd never heard before: "bio-family." This was meant to indicate the family we were born into, not necessarily the family we were called into.

"We can honor our biological families without betraying who God has called us to be," Les argued passionately. His right hand was constantly in a salute position, with the thumb tucked under the straight fingers. The more passionate he became, the more emphasis he put on it. "He's brought us together with a reason. We're on this ship, and we promise to never let each other go. And that's going to ruffle some feathers,"—he laughed—"because that's not how the world does things! But we're not here to gratify the man. "We are here to please God."

On Christmas morning, a swarm of people walked around the house, preparing and trading plates, pouring juice and coffee; someone wanted plain pancakes, while another preferred blueberry. Les fried up a large amount of bacon, half of which was consumed by the Barbarians. Ed, Pam, and Harker were the only ones who didn't eat meat, so Pam prepared a cornflake and cottage cheese dish (which was still intact by the end of the night). Miguel and Juana brought their four-year-old daughter, and the three of them walked outside with Emily, Lucy, and Brandon to make snowmen. Harker read his Bible on the living room floor, Mina and Jasmine studied the Welsh prophet's book on the couch, QB played video games, and Dontay desperately tried to solve a Rubik's Cube. It was everything I wanted in a family vacation.
"Who did you get as Secret Santa?Dontay questioned me. These were the only gifts we'd be exchanging, and Les' concept was that they should all be unique. Custom-made for the person whose name you choose.
"Do not answer that!" Jasmine said, swatting him. "You shouldn't ask them that. What if it is you!?"
"It's not me," Dontay reassured. "She has been walking around with pink paint on her hands!" Joie, have you made me anything pink?"
I gazed up at Dontay from the beanbag chair I'd slumped into, picking at the pink paint remnants from the mixed-media collage I'd just finished for Emily. "Nope." I said with a smile. "Not for you."
He extended his tongue at Jasmine, who rolled her eyes.
I appreciated their siblinglike conduct. They had both been living in the residence for about a year. Unlike those of us in Los Angeles, they were members of Les' true inner circle. Some evenings, Jasmine and Dontay would even sneak into the master bedroom, welcomed to watch TV with Les, Marti, and the boys, where The Sopranos was a constant presence. It was Les' favourite show. He could identify to Tony since he was constantly under attack from outside forces and did all it took to keep his family together. I wasn't a fan of the

program back then—too much "tough Jersey" stuff I didn't want to see again—but I was content to sit and journal. But sometimes I wished I had been invited.

Suddenly, the supersized beanbag I was sitting on collapsed around me, lifting me off the ground. I could hear Les and Quiet Boy laughing as I was wrapped tighter and tighter. I was unable to move since it was so tight. I had intense, visceral panic. And then I experienced a quick succession of flashbacks: three nurses putting me in a straitjacket so the doctor could stitch up a gash under my brow caused by a living-room acrobatics incident. The actor who portrayed Boo Radley to my Scout in the regional production of To Kill a Mockingbird threw me up in the air in an outdoor pool in Texas. My parents parted during the summer. Was he trying to date my mother? He then gave me a gold ID bracelet with his name on it. A seventh-grade boy pushed me against a chain-link fence and held a metal bat to my throat because he was angry with me for ignoring him. An 11:00 p.m. Meeting with director James Toback in his editing bay, naively thinking I was helping him out by meeting him late because he was on a long shoot, only to be paralyzed for an hour listening to him verbally undress me, saying things like "Every woman likes to be licked a different way." A young man in New York who was a member of my church violently lifting and holding me against a wall on the street while our friends watched. He squeezed his body against mine and hissed, with hot breath, "You'd better not talk like that unless you're ready to do something about it." I'm not sure what I responded, but I recall our entire group of friends doing nothing but waiting for it to stop.

Les and QB were giggling. Everybody was laughing.

"One, two, three!"" QB said, and I was in the air for a second, before landing back on the bag they were carrying. They wrapped me up again, getting a firm grasp on the bag.

"One, two, three!""

Oh, this is a game! I realized. They are playing with me. They are not trying to harm me. They are playing. Like family. There is no cause to be terrified.

The fear I was feeling dissipated, the flashbacks faded, and I started laughing. I laughed so hard that my eyes wet. I looked up as I landed safely on the ground again. QB smiled. Les and Dontay were chuckling.

I've always wanted brothers.
Les tousled my hair. "You looked like you could use some shaking up," he told you.
I stood up and threw my arms around him, sobbing.
"Oh no, I am sorry, baby; did we injure you? "We were just playing."
"No, it's not that." I pawed at my face. "I simply feel so cherished. "The only thing I've ever wanted was a large family like this."
Les hugged me back. "You are family, Joy. You belong here." Even if those weren't the perfect words, that Christmas seemed more important than any I'd ever had—thanks in large part to Secret Santa. Instead of being shuffled around to extended bio-family and subjected to the obligatory fawning over impersonal gifts like socks or a new Costco blender, this Family exchanged gifts that had been painstakingly crafted for each individual: a knitted sweater, a painting of someone's favorite childhood memory, custom jewelry. The amount of work and effort put into these was extraordinary.
That night, on my bunk, I examined my Secret Santa gift. It was from the QB. He had made me a little wooden box, burned my name and a rose into the top, and secured it with a lock; inside was a hand-bound diary with flower-adorned paper he had molded and pressed from pulp. It must have taken several months. It didn't seem romantic to me at the time since I saw him as a brother, but I felt seen and cared for. I fell asleep thinking about the next time I could return to Idaho. I would have remained longer, but January in LA is pilot season.

PART TWO

CHAPTER TWELVE

"I really think you should reconsider," my manager remarked from behind the desk in her Los Feliz office. "This pilot has a lot of buzz."
A few days prior, she had sent me a script for Ravens, a Warner Bros. teen drama pilot. I skimmed through it without reading much.
High school, basketball, stupid jokes about sticky magazine pages, angry female, dull best friend, teens having sex...eh.
"I don't want to be stuck on a teen soap," I informed her. "Especially not after two years with Guiding Light. I want to make films. I'm a talented actress who wants to express meaningful stories and collaborate with the finest of the best.
"YOU WILL. You're consistently down to the last few women on major studio films. I believe a position like this can only help you get over the hump."
I began working with my manager while on Guiding Light. She believed in me so much that she would—and had to—walk into every casting office that refused to give me a chance.
"But no one on TV does film," I explained. Which was correct. Before streaming, movie stars wouldn't appear on an American TV show unless it was a cameo on Friends, and very good TV stars couldn't get a role in a movie for fear their "little-box fame" would taint the film's grandeur.
"There are actors starting to cross over from TV to film," my manager stated.
"Who?"
"Jennifer Aniston."
"She's the most famous woman in the world."
"Katie Holmes, Michelle Williams, Keri Russell..."
"Katie, OK. However, Michelle only appears in independent films. I haven't seen Keri in any movies."
"Keri was just in We Were Soldiers, the Mel Gibson one."
I exhaled. "Did she get that?" Damn that. "I enjoyed that role."
"See."
"But they were all leads on their shows," I corrected myself. "This Ravens part is just a side character."
"I think it's gonna be a real ensemble show," she told me.
Historically, I jumped at the opportunity to perform any type of work. But suddenly, as I was attempting to "break free" from the old

narrative of being second best, accepting a supporting role in what I thought was a teen soap felt like a spiritual test. Do I truly believe that God has better things for me, or will I continue to believe a lie?

"Listen," I replied. "I've been sitting in New York casting offices with Anne, Scarlett, Kirsten, and Natalie since I was twelve years old, and their names still appear on the sign-in page for screen tests I attend. Julia Stiles cannot be accessible for everything. Let's simply wait. "It will happen."

"Okay," my manager replied. "You understand what you want. The WB adores you. There will be others.

And there was soon. I cast the female lead in a superhero pilot written by Mr. & Mrs. Smith's Simon Kinberg for megaproducer Jerry Bruckheimer. Ironically, Camille was cast in this role initially, and I was next in line when she had to refuse due to schedule issues. Sure, technically this violated my "no settling for second best" commitment, but I regarded it as an exemption because I was filling in for Camille, and it seemed more destined by God. Also, a female has to eat. It was a massive TV show with a large budget and a lot of buzz because no one had done superheroes before. After the pilot was shot, the buzz on the street was that this show will definitely be picked up. Then, like so many others, it didn't.

With this discouragement, I pressed even harder on the Family in LA, despite the fact that we were going through some upheavals. Now that Mina had her kid, she and Harker were ready to relocate to Idaho full-time; Abe was focusing more and more on his band; and Les was not visiting LA as frequently as before. He called on a regular basis to check on me and the other members of the group, but because he had begun to construct a formal "ministry" vision for the Idaho "Big House Family," as we had all jokingly dubbed it, he didn't have as much time to visit. Pam naturally took on the position of leader/mother to everyone in the LA group, including a few new ladies who had joined us, such as Emily's younger sister and Gretchen's twin cousins.

Since Les couldn't come down to LA, everyone began scheduling regular visits up north, but Camille was the only one who never showed up. In reality, we'd been seeing her less and less. She was a popular professional actress who was frequently on site for assignments, so I assumed that was why. But one day, we went to lunch, and the truth was revealed.

Her parents had been in town the week before, and they joined us at the Whisky a Go Go for Abe's band concert. Halfway through the set, the band took a break, and I caught a glimpse of Pam exchanging some unpleasant words with Camille's mother. But, unlike Pam and my mother's birthday conversation, the conflict was brief, and Pam was soon smiling and talking to Emily, so I didn't think much of it.

"Honestly, it was pretty weird, Joie," Camille replied, moving the salad around her plate. "My mom was just asking her about what her role was in the church—"

"Wait, does she know that it's not... like, we don't have a church?"

"Yes, but I believe that is also part of the confusion. "Who is in charge?"

"No one," I said, just as I had informed my father on the phone earlier. Why did everyone keep asking about this? "We're just friends meeting and doing life together."

"But there are leaders."

"Well, I suppose. Harker and Abe sort of lead it, and I'd say Ed and Pam are our spiritual parents here. Les and Marti will represent the group in Idaho."

She squeezed her face sideways and pressed her lips together. "Well, it absolutely began with Harker and Abe simply offering their home to anybody who were curious about God and wanted to pray and such. But, Joie, it has not been like that for a long time. Les and Pam have clearly seized control. And what exactly are 'spiritual parents'?

"I do not see it as a takeover. I see them as being really selfless and willing to take on those natural parental duties for all of us. Spiritual parents essentially fill up the gaps where our biological parents failed to raise and lead us.

"'Bio-parents'?"

Camille had never heard of this term before because she had not spent Christmas in Idaho.

"Yes, you know, biological parents and families. We have been adopted into God's kingdom, thus the families we were born into are not always the ones who should have authority in our life. Pam and Les feel more like parents to me than my own."

Camille contemplated it. "I guess I understand how—since there's so much drama with your parents—how maybe it's really helpful to have older figures who will care about you in that way."

"Yes, it's a huge blessing!"

"But I have a good relationship with my parents." My family isn't perfect, but I don't need spiritual parents. "I have parents.
"If your parents don't know Jesus, how can they...?" I'm talking about spiritual discernment. "If they don't have a relationship with God, they can't give you sound advice."
"Well, I don't know if you have to be a person of faith in order to have wisdom—"
I shut her off. "It says in the Bible that wisdom comes from God."
"But they do have a relationship with God."
"They do?"
"I was raised Catholic."
"Yes, but that is religion. That is not moving with the Holy Spirit."
She shook her head and exhaled. "Look, all I know is that my mother was attempting to ask Pam for additional information about the Bible study, such as who is in charge, what authors they're teaching, who Les is, and what his qualifications are. So, did he attend seminary? Pam became very closed off and began speaking to my mother as if she were an enemy. It seemed so strange."
"That doesn't sound like Pam."
"Well, Mom attempted to reassure her that she is just trying to understand since I am her daughter and she adores me. Pam responded, 'She's our daughter, too, and we love her.'" Camille halted, and her eyes widened. "Like, come on, that's kinda creepy— telling someone's mother that she's actually your child instead?"
"I..." I wasn't sure what to say. "Are you sure your mom heard her correctly? "We were at a club."
"She said Pam was very clear."
"I don't know, Cam." Honestly? "I just..." "I don't believe Pam said that." I shrugged apologetically. I've known her for nearly two years. She's always been quite lovely and consistent, and—"
"My mom wouldn't randomly lie about that."
"She must have misunderstood, then," I decided.
We sat quietly at the table, neither of our meals being disturbed.
She shook her head and gazed down. "I think I'm just gonna take a break from Bible study."
I couldn't believe we were here; God had taken us both this far, and she was going to leave.
"Doesn't this seem like the enemy is just getting exactly what he wants?" "I said." "You've come so far; your prayer life is flourishing,

and incredible little miracles are happening all the time. Are you really going to give that up because of a misunderstanding?"
Camille stared at me with much grief and pity. At the time, I assumed it was for herself—for not being strong and courageous enough to completely give her life to God. Now I know it was for me.
"If you want to talk or hang out, you know I love you and we're fine..." That's just not the best place for me right now."
We finished lunch with a final hug and parted ways. I would not see her again for two years.

CHAPTER THIRTEEN

In June, I received another contact from my manager regarding Ravens, the TV series I had turned down. It had been picked up and given a new title: One Tree Hill. They were recasting a role and asked expressly for me.
"It starts shooting in ten days in North Carolina, and I think she'd be perfect for this part," the casting director told my manager. "Can you please ask her to reconsider and come read for us?"
I remained determined to pursue a career in movies. I knew I had a thousand distinct characters inside of me, with a hundred various ways to play them. I wanted to learn and play in the major leagues, but this television job felt like Little League. I also wanted to work. Where was the line between being appreciative for every chance and staying true to my own vision? I did not know. I prayed for discernment, decided to let God make the decision, and informed my manager that I would take the audition.
I waited in the waiting area with a really attractive brunette who was listening to the great new iPod that everyone was raving about while concentrating on her script pages. She smiled nicely at me and returned to her job. I was escorted into a bright room beside the show's creator and a few other people. I read my scenes for the girl-next-door role they had initially approached me about, and it went quite well. The writing was enjoyable and easy to read, the conversation was natural, and I felt at ease in the role of Haley James. Just as I was about to depart, the casting director shocked me by asking if I would read for a new role they were writing: a "vixen

next door." Suddenly, all of my internal Christian-purity-culture bells went off. I was trying to be the best version of myself right now. Innocent. Childlike.

Oh, no. The enemy is attempting to capture me. How can I be a good Christian while playing the sexpot?

I read it to them but gave a poor performance on purpose in the hopes that they would only consider me for the first job. I didn't have to worry. I never had a legitimate shot at that vixen character. The casting director was undoubtedly attempting to employ a good actress to demonstrate to the showrunner that no one would be better suited for that dynamite role than the lovely, headphone-wearing brunette I had just met.

The screen exam was conducted two days later. Things were going quickly because filming for season one would start within a week. In most cases, the screen test is the final step after a series of callbacks before landing the job. Your contract is arranged before you arrive, and your episodic price is always based on your previous paychecks from other shows. Every work raises an actor's "quote," which is a strange contradiction for actors like me who, while still considered unknown, had higher quotations due to all the grounded TV pilots we'd shot. Do we accept a reduced compensation to make ourselves more desirable to the studio's budget? Or do we keep the income we've earned and hope that the studio values us? It's a gamble on yourself, knowing that if they can get a different actor for less money, they will—so if you keep to your quotation (as I did), you'd better bring something truly unique to the screen test.

This screen test also acted as a "chemistry read," which means you were placed in a room with ten executives in seats and an actor who had previously been cast. The Suits are trying to determine if you look well together on camera and if you have that elusive, non-manufacturable quality that keeps everyone watching their show.

One of those execs (who, to this day, I have never seen wearing a suit) called my manager the night before the screen test. He was also in charge of another project I'd been invited to test a year before: Amanda Bynes' What I Like About You. I had turned down the invitation. The show was marketed to tween girls, and I was concerned that the big-sister part I was auditioning for—which was finally played by the gorgeous Jennie Garth—was a woman living with her boyfriend. I did not want to popularize "living in sin" among young girls.

After my manager finished speaking with this executive, she called me.

"I have a direct quote that I've been asked to relay to you," she told me, "to make sure you know exactly what you're getting into before you sign this contract."

"Okayyy," I replied cautiously.

"He said, 'You tell her this show is about fucking and sucking, and if she's gonna have a problem with that, she shouldn't come in tomorrow.'"

My manager hesitated. I wasn't sure what to say. She didn't either.

"So," she finally said, "what do you think?"

I'd seen the pilot. It was clearly influenced by 8 Mile, the recent Eminem-Brittany Murphy film that was nasty and vulgar, but which I genuinely like because of how real the anguish was. Despite my early experience as a singing songbook sidekick, I despised "Christian" films. They dealt with tragedy and pain in an overly simplistic manner, without the complexities and depth of real life. I believed it was critical that stories depict relatable darkness and hardship because, to me, this is where redemption may take place. So, grit did not intimidate me, and the One Tree Hill pilot possessed grit.

The show was about two half-brothers who went to high school in the small town of Tree Hill. One brother was the son of a single mother. Even though they lived paycheck to paycheck, they were content. This sibling was a reader and poet, but he was also an excellent basketball player, a talent he acquired from his father. His father still resided in town, but in a more prosperous neighborhood with his wife and second son by a minute. This brother was a basketball superstar and the most popular child in town. The brothers fought over a gorgeous, gloomy girl. Her best friend provided hot comedic relief. I'd be the awkward girl next door.

The characters in the pages I had read were well-developed. I felt my role was the most wholesome of them all, so I wasn't concerned about being objectified. One thing I was certain of: I was not in Hollywood to create Christian films. I wanted to tell true stories. One Tree Hill felt apart from other bubble-gum TV shows with hidden intentions. I believed in the show's ability to convey relevant, inspiring messages to the audience.

"Just tell him I understand what he's saying," I said to my manager. "I'm not going to try to stop them from writing about actual teenagers. I believe in the show and want to be a part of it.

The screen test was conducted at the Warner Bros. Ranch in North Hollywood. I have been screen-testing there since high school. Selma Blair went in after me to screen Zoe, Duncan, Jack, and Jane. Her water bottle began dripping all over her hands just as she entered the testing room, and I remember thinking, Damn. That's ideal for this character. She'll completely get this. And she did.

The ranch was less formal than the massive, gated WB studio land a few blocks away. Little casting and production huts dot the manicured walks of flowers and curved topiaries. Going there always seemed wonderful, knowing that I was producing art, if only for a minute, in the same location where some of my favorite childhood shows, such as Bewitched and I Dream of Jeannie, were shot. When I had time after tests or auditions, I would drive about and gaze at the old sets, which were kept like monuments, as well as the new ones that were being built. This time, however, I didn't linger. I parked toward the far edge of the lot to give myself time for a thinking walk, drawing lines as I carefully approached the screen-test building I'd been walking into for years.

I signed in and was promptly led into the testing room by a casting assistant. I waved to everyone, as was customary. There are no hugs here.

"Hi, this is Joie Lenz. She's reading to Haley. Joie, this is Chad Michael Murray. He'll be reading beside you.

This guy Chad was apparently already well-known, with recurring roles on Gilmore Girls and Dawson's Creek, but I didn't watch much TV at the time, so I wasn't in a position to be impressed by him except for his compelling performance in the pilot as Lucas Scott, the bookish-secret-sports-star-from-the-wrong-side-of-the-tracks. He was tall yet bent and shy. Then he smoldered at me as he shook both of my hands. Was he doing Brando? It's funny how I'd jump out of a moving cab in New York to get a guy this handsome to notice me, but here at work, I just assumed he had something in his eyes. I could understand why he was becoming a celebrity. He had everything he needed to tape up a bedroom wall.

"Hi, Joie, thank you so much for coming in today."

I smiled back and said the appropriate thing: "Oh my gosh, of course, thank you for having me!"

This was a dance of politeness that everyone in LA appeared to perform. I preferred the practicality of New York casting directors and performers, who may thank you for coming in as a gesture of professional civility, but only in the same manner that one might thank a mailman for dropping off a box. The questions, answers, and kind exchanges were genuine. New Yorkers value time and are primarily concerned with completing tasks successfully. If you perform a good job, they will thank you lavishly. If you're a cool person who works hard, they'll keep inviting you back. It was really straightforward.

Los Angeles social cues confused me. The way people interacted had so many time-wasting layers. Hi, unemployed, unknown actor who has been invited into one of the most elite rooms where everyone here has the power to give you the life you've always wanted. Let me show you how humble I am by thanking you for sacrificing your time, even though we both know this is literally the only place in the world you want to be. I just want to make sure you leave this experience knowing that I'm amazing.

Oh, but no! Allow me to show you how humble I am by expressing how lucky I feel to be invited into your presence. It is I who am grateful. And you are too kind to even imagine I would rather be somewhere else. Also, if I don't get this job, I just want to make sure you know that I know you're amazing, so maybe you'll give me a different job some other time. Then we can talk more about how amazing we both are!

After all this sucralose, the rejection of not finding a job in LA always hurt more than it did in New York, since I am a person who believes in others.

To be fair, Chad's tenderness was genuine, as I would come to discover. I'd always hated how in Hollywood auditions, you had to play a scene before it began.

There was a cafeteria lunch table and two chairs near our seats that we could sit in or not. They rolled the camera, and when I looked at this sandy-blond-haired guy who was meant to be my high school closest buddy, Blue Eyes was the obvious emotional parallel. Any nerves I had vanished when I realized all I had to do now was remember any number of summer days with him, our feet dangling off the lake pier.

I pushed the chairs out of the way and sprang up to sit on top of the table like a bench. This resulted in a modest but noticeable alteration in the room's energy. There was a slight sound of individuals pushing forward in their chairs. I thought I heard a chuckle. Clearly, no one who had auditioned had made this move. Chad smiled, glad I wanted to participate and have fun. That's how acting is supposed to be. That is why the majority of us started doing it. Nothing beats pretend play. However, once you start doing it professionally, the key is to avoid becoming lost in your ego and forgetting how. However, attempting to become more childlike in my spiritual life enabled me to become more childlike in my acting life. Chad immediately joined me at the table, where we began the scene.

HALEY: *Did you ever figure out your porn name?*
LUCAS: *What are you talking about?*
HALEY: *Your porn name. Um, you know, you take the name of your first pet and your mother's maiden name and you put them together. What was the name of your first pet?*
LUCAS: *You know that. I had a dog named Rocket.*
HALEY: *Oh, Rocket! Ah! I loved Rocket. [Pause] So your mother's maiden name is Roe. Rocket Roe! [Laughs] Nice.*
LUCAS: *What's yours?*
HALEY: *Uh, oh, I had a bunny, named Bunny.*
LUCAS: *You had a bunny named Bunny?*
HALEY: *Yes, I did. And my mother's maiden name is Beaugard. So...*
LUCAS: *Bunny Beaugard.*
HALEY: *Dawson's Freak. Starring Rocket Roe and Bunny Beaugard.*
LUCAS: *Nice.*
HALEY: *Shut up!*

At this point, I kicked Chad sideways with my foot. Boom. The energy in the room altered even more. I believe that because Chad was famous, the other girls reading with him were scared or hesitant to touch him. These executives had been seeing this scene repeatedly, but when our bodies literally connected, they all woke up. Sometimes all it takes to get a job is to do something that gets everyone's attention. So I leaned into it, and for the rest of the scenario, I treated Chad like a younger brother.

HALEY: *Hey, um, this game tonight. You're not playing anymore?*
LUCAS: *No. [Pause] You know I've never walked away from anything before, Haley?*
HALEY: *Yeah.*
LUCAS: *But I can't do it. And even worse, I don't know why I can't do it. You know, it's like, no matter how confusing or screwed up life got, the game always made sense. It was mine, you know. And in a lot of ways it's who I am. But I can't be that person in their gym, or in their uniforms, or... in their world.*

I'd read these lines a hundred times before, but it wasn't until I was in the room that I saw the comparison between Lucas's situation and my own. It seemed as if I were speaking to myself. And with Chad there as a tangible embodiment of my inner struggle, I felt compelled to offer myself solace in a way I hadn't been able to do in months. I reached out and wrapped my arm around him.

HALEY: *I hear you, Luke. But I know you. And I know that no matter what happens you're still going to be the same guy you always were. No uniform, no... whatever, is gonna ruin that, you know?*

Chad grinned at me. However, Chad was no longer Chad. This was no longer a fantasy. We had arrived at that uncommon but highly sought-after moment in acting when the performance became reality. A form of transubstantiation. Joy and Chad transformed into Haley and Lucas for those brief moments at a cafeteria table altar. I hesitated, jumped up from the table, and tousled his hair.

HALEY: *Call me later. We'll go get some pizza.*

He laughed and shoved my hand away, and we made faces before I went away.

I sensed something extraordinary had just happened, but if the Suits knew, they didn't say anything as we exchanged thank-yous, goodbyes, and other gag-inducing politesse.

As I headed back to my car, I heard someone call out, "Joie!" I turned to see Chad jogging across the parking lot toward me. Now that our job was finished, I could appreciate his looks more, however seeing him jogging reminded me of Dontay sprinting the softball bases and made me long for the next opportunity to see him in Idaho—my crush had grown gradually over the prior few months.

"Hey!" I replied. "Did I leave something in there?"

"No," Chad answered. "I just wanted to congratulate and welcome you to the show! You absolutely nailed it in there."

He came in for a hug. I wasn't sure what to say. I'd never had an actor walk out of a screen test and immediately tell me I got the role. That was left to producers, managers, and attorneys to argue over before someone won the prize of calling the actor with the exciting news. The show's headliner personally informed me that I had been hired. I felt a rush of exhilaration, but I'd been in this profession long enough to know that nothing is genuine until it's filmed. Even then, you could end up on the cutting room floor or have the entire film shelved. I knew better than to get enthusiastic, but I thanked Chad and hoped everything worked well.

The following morning, I received a phone call from my manager: I will be leaving for Wilmington, North Carolina in five days.

Over the next week, I was filled with dread about leaving my new spiritual family. It was a series pickup, which meant twenty-two episodes, eight days each—the next nine months of my life were dedicated to this new project.

I'm not prepared for this! I am simply relearning how to be a kid. I'm trying to heal. Why did I put myself in this situation? Why did I say yes in the first place? I've been on my own for a long time, and now that I have a family, I don't want to go out alone again!

Les and Marti called to congratulate me: "We've heard the news! Sounds like a wonderful job, and we wanted you to know we're rooting for you!"

My automobile would be picked up and sent the morning of my flight. I handed Emily my apartment key in case anyone wanted to use it again for a prayer retreat, packed a few suitcases, and prepared my mind and heart to depart.

The Bible study group met for a farewell supper at Coco's, a chain restaurant on LA's outskirts. The Van Hewitts, who had previously been Seventh-day Adventists, had less than discerning taste sensibilities, and Coco's—one step up from a diner—was their favorite go-to destination. I knew well than to complain. When Les and the Barbarians were in town, I tried to divert us to sushi. He made a joke about how demanding I was.

Sweet Ed asked if he might pray for me in the parking lot, after passing up the majority of my country fried steak. I admired Ed's prayers since they were always hesitant. I could identify to the uneasiness that came with talking to God out loud in front of others. I value that attribute even more now that I understand what a red signal it is when someone is really comfortable improvising complex prayers. That was not Ed. He lived in Pam's shadow, silent and often alone. So when he volunteered to pray, I knew he meant it.

"Lord, we are humbled to be here to encourage your daughter Joy—"

"Your precious daughter," Pam interrupted.

Ed hesitated and then resumed. "Thank you for caring about us and listening. Thank you for giving Joy the opportunity to get to know you better in a different setting. Kindly keep her safe. Wishing her safe travels... My eyes were closed, but we were holding hands, and I could feel him bouncing on his toes while thinking. "...give her permission to be excited."

The group responded with "yeses" and "amens." Everyone else prayed as well, which is an embarrassing practice in many charismatic gatherings where everyone is expected to pray because refusing to talk to God is a terrible look. As a result, it took almost 35 minutes to break the late-night hand-holding circle and exit the parking lot of this lousy chain restaurant in the central valley. Emily handed me a diary with Bible verses inscribed on the pages, Pam gave me a card with an overly sappy message, and I climbed into my car, finally alone.

Driving back to my place, I reflected on the final sentence of Ed's prayer, and my nervousness turned to exhilaration.

Who is this Haley James? Does she have a southern accent? How does she walk? Is she a fast talker or slow talker? Do her ears stick out? I could put some bobby pins behind my ears to make them poke out—that would be cute! Does she have blonde hair like mine? Or should it be brown? The other actress from the pilot is blonde, maybe I should change to brunette. Where is she insecure and where is she confident? What kind of family did she grow up in? Is she clumsy? Is she goofy? Is she studious and quiet? I had so many questions. So many ideas.

I spent the next day of flying, including a connection and layover, busily writing down as many questions and character creations as I could think of. At last, I arrived at Wilmington.

CHAPTER FOURTEEN

August in a southern seaside town means just one thing. Hot. Like in a difficult Hitchcock thriller, the sun has moved closer to the earth, and Vera Miles is dragging herself to the city's final operating water fountain. As I stepped out of the airport, a humid bulk from the Atlantic burrowed into my bones. I exhaled as deeply as possible, the weight of water and salt on my chest transporting me back to my boyhood in Florida. Amazingly, my skin was moist in less than ten seconds. Inside the car, I asked the driver if we could turn off the air conditioning and roll down the windows. He smiled at me in the rearview mirror, thinking it was a joke. When he realized it wasn't, his smile faded and he rolled down the windows. He drove far faster than the speed limit on his way to the studio, where I was scheduled for a wardrobe fitting.

We entered the EUE/Screen Gems Studios in downtown

Wilmington. Frank Capra Jr. owned these famed stages, and his father was the famous 1930s and 1940s film director of It's a Wonderful Life, Arsenic & Old Lace, and Hollywood's first rom-com, It Happened One Night. Capra Jr. aimed to create a Hollywood East with cheaper production expenses and to capitalize on the historic little town and beach beauty. One Tree Hill would take over the filming stages from Dawson's Creek, but Screen Gems has previously hosted films such as Empire Records, Crimes of the Heart, Blue Velvet, 28 Days, A Walk to Remember, and Drew Barrymore's Firestarter. Interestingly, it was also the location where Brandon Lee died in an on-set accident while filming The Crow.

I was used to the LA studios that towered over everything and whose manicured garden walks were trodden by executives on their way to important meetings in buildings decorated with nicely framed movie posters and cappuccino machines. This was significantly more basic, with six low-ceilinged stages on blacktop, a gravel lot for trailers, and no flowers. Staff and crew were all familiar with one another after filming the pilot and spending a month in preproduction. In the production office, with its walls covered in mood boards and actors' headshots, I was greeted with smiles and sweet tea, followed by surprised stares when I requested them to call me "Joy" despite the fact that the production sheet said "Bethany."

Prior to my arrival, I had determined that as part of my dedication to "becoming who God made me to be," I would neither volunteer at a soup kitchen or construct houses with Habitat for Humanity, but instead use my birth name. "Joie"—the nickname I'd adopted at thirteen and by which everyone knew me professionally—was what was preventing me from moving forward! I built a false self in an attempt to make myself unique. In spite of acting as an idol in my life, I decided to toss away all of my professional credits from the previous 10 years and go by my full name: "Bethany Joy Lenz." At least, that's how I wanted it to appear in the show's credits. But on set, I still wanted people to call me "Joy."

A production assistant led me to my trailer, the front half of a double banger, which I promptly decorated with insane amounts of Target merchandise. On my way to meet with hair and makeup, I came across a tall boy with black hair whom I had seen in the pilot. Teen shows like this one were known for casting actors who were significantly older than their characters. Gabrielle Carteris was twenty-nine when she began as sixteen-year-old Andrea Zuckerman on Beverly Hills, 90210. According to my manager, our cast's age difference was not as significant. The majority of the actors were in their early twenties. But this youngster had to be a real teenager.

"Oh, hey, I'm James Lafferty," he added, pausing to shake my hand. James portrayed Nathan Scott, the privileged half-brother.

"Hi, my name is Joy, and I'm playing Haley," I clarified. "You were great in the pilot."

"It's nice to meet you! Did you say Julie?"

"Joy. Bethany. But"—now reciting this for the seventy-third time and regretting my decision—"Joy is my middle name, and everyone calls me Joy."

"Oh, I get it. Well, Joy, welcome to the show! Hopefully, we'll be able to get some scenes together!"

Oh, we'd have plenty. Neither of us realized it at the time, but our characters would marry in high school and become one of the most popular TV couples in pop culture history.

For now, we were just strangers in the heat. The PA who was showing me around overheard something on her radio earpiece and activated the small black box microphone connected to her shirt. She looked up at James and said, "Copy that." "New basketball coordinator is here to meet you."

"Okay, I'll see you soon!"" James said, hurrying away.

I waved goodbye and entered into the chilly air of the hair and makeup trailer.

As with many productions, this trailer served as the nerve center of the entire operation, as it was the only location where every performer had to stop before entering set. Hair and cosmetics are continually evolving organisms. The ambiance of the room shifts depending on the scene that is going to be filmed. There were mornings when I walked in and Motown was playing and three people were waiting because the six chairs were already full of performers, some half-dressed and everyone talking. Other times, I'd go in and find silence, but for the dull drone of a single blow dryer, as a lone actor prepared to film an emotional moment with no interruptions. This was the hallowed spot where all hidden chats took place. There were no microphones inside, so whispers could easily be lost in the noise. This was where we would see the raw, true versions of each other before the makeup was applied, before the hangover passed, after the split, and after the on-set argument—all of which were more likely given our youth. To me, the women who operated this trailer were the Mama Bears because of their readiness to listen, ability to keep secrets, and wisdom they shared—along with plenty of dirty jokes and the occasional hidden bottle of tequila.

I reached for the cheery, freckled hair department key, but was pulled into a great hug.

"Welcome to the show!!!"" she said in a charming, tight tone.

The remaining Mama Bears followed suit. The routine of hugs reminded me of the Big House and made me sad, but there was little time for that as I was hustled into a chair and brushed, scrutinized, color-matched, and questioned.

"Oh, your hair's curly. We'll need to straighten it. Are you opposed going brunette? Split the ends. "Let us trim you up."

"What is your skin type?" You have an olive skin tone, therefore you could be combination but lean oily. How well does your skin keep makeup in humid conditions?"

The outfit designer also stopped by to worry over me.

"Do you think Haley dresses more antique or like the Gap? Hourglass figure. Are you certain you're twenty-six in jeans?"

I stared as they buzzed about me. Pat, pat, pat, with a couple of brand-new straws. That is how we keep you young and fair in the merry old Oz. I was happy to go along with everything. We were developing a character. Creating something from nothing. There was magic in the making.

The next day, we did a table read with the entire cast during lunchtime. I sat next two 1990s heartthrobs, Paul Johansson and Craig Sheffer. Paul was a big deal on television in the 1990s, and he played Dan Scott, the father of the half brothers at the heart of the plot. He also reminded me of Dontay: he was the same imposing size, but more Canadian lumberjack than college footballer. Craig had previously acted in Some Kind of Wonderful and A River Runs Through It with Brad Pitt, and now he played Dan Scott's brother, Uncle Keith. He had a gruff look, similar to Paul's, but solely in denim, which worked well for him. I also formed feelings for him, which Paul would later relentlessly mock. Craig's first words to me after doing a double take under the bright fluorescent lights were, "Whoa, you look like a monster!"This is always encouraging for a young woman to hear. We laughed about it, and then I met more producers, hugged Chad, waved to James, and shook hands with Hilarie Burton. Hilarie's career began as an on-air personality for MTV. It was her first serious part. She was portraying Peyton Sawyer, the girl that the two brothers were battling over. Though she was considerably more joyful and self-assured than her persona, Hilarie exuded a similar magnetic aura that pulled everyone in: she was already everyone's sister; one of the males with no competitive streak toward the girls. I liked her immediately away.

The only person I avoided at the table was Moira Kelly, one of my acting heroes from the rom-com classic The Cutting Edge, whom I had seen more times than I could count. She performed opposite Robert Downey Jr. in Chaplin before moving on to The West Wing. She was now playing the mother of Lucas Scott. I'd had a paralysis of desire since I was a child. The more I want something, the more afraid I grew. There was the risk that I would receive what I desired only to fail and discover that I am unworthy of it. There was also the risk that I would not receive what I desired, demonstrating that I am unworthy of it. The fact that she was in the show reinforced for me that it had substance. I wanted Moira to be my mentor, to teach me everything she knew about the craft of acting, but I was so afraid she'd say no, or that if she said yes, I'd disappoint her, that I simply shook her hand, said hello, and observed her from a distance for the next ten years.

As the weeks passed, the cast and crew spent time getting to know one another, finding ways to interact, determining who got along and who didn't, and anthropologically categorizing ourselves as nerdy, jock-y, gourmand, debaucherous, old, whimsical, and religious (guess who). We connected with whoever shared our sensibilities.

Hilarie and I were a nerdy-whimsical mix, with a strong emphasis on the whimsy. We talked endlessly about our childhood love of Shelley Duvall's '80s TV show Faerie Tale Theatre, cited Sondheim, read poems, and drove around Wilmington antiquing. We both collected unusual items such as taxidermy and Victorian mourning lockets with human hair inside. She also enjoyed crafting and was always upcycling old items. I once entered my trailer and found a gift from her: a Macallan 10 whisky box painted in bronze acrylic, ornamented with a glued-on flea-market photo, and covered in an original poetry written with metallic marker. She blossomed around my heart like a

honeysuckle vine, and I was grateful for the sense of sisterhood.
Despite being late to the production, I was not the last cast member to arrive. At the table read for the third episode, the attractive iPod girl from my audition entered. Sophia Bush played Brooke Davis, Peyton's humorous best friend. Sophia was also amusing and mischievous, always up for an impulsive adventure. Shortly after arriving in Wilmington, she asked me to accompany her to pick up a pit bull puppy that someone was selling. We drove two hours through North Carolina. On the way back, we had not only the pitbull puppy, but also a golden Lab puppy that I had purchased, caught up in the moment. That night, I slept over at her apartment, and the four of us crowded into her brand-new, spotless white bed. The next morning, we awoke to the bright sun on us with puppy poo all over the bed. We were having fits of laughter.
"I thought you raised a lot of dogs growing up!"I said.
"Well, my folks did." She cackled with the throaty husk that would soon make her famous, and we stripped her bed as the dogs battled on the floor.
A few weeks later, I realized I wasn't prepared to raise a hyper dog while working long hours, so I found her a great family with a farm to live on. I also quickly realized I wasn't prepared to get too close to Sophia. She was not just effervescent and caring, but also extremely brilliant. She had the type of brain that kept track of everyday events on a mental spreadsheet or could read Carl Sagan's Cosmos and tell you that "We make our world significant by the courage of our questions and the depth of our answers" was on page 120, at the end of the fourth paragraph. NASA might have used her intelligence, but she's so lovely that astronauts wouldn't want to leave Earth. She reminded me of how I felt about Blue Eyes' family and cheerleader. Sophia was a Nantucket girl, and I was trying hard not to experience the pain of that comparison again.
I failed to see that she was also working hard. Sophia was frequently favored and constantly underestimated in life due of her beauty—a character characteristic that made her ideal for the role of Brooke Davis but conflicted with my own fears and militant convictions about how one should prove their value. I missed the irony that I was doing the exact same thing, but with religion as my baseline. My growing friendship with sweet Sophia became a casualty of this, and instead of sitting shiva for my ego, I really fucking wish I could go

back in time, walk into her trailer, and hug her long and hard.

The only persons on set who I was certain were Christians were two wardrobe girls and the driver who picked me up from the airport and shuttled me to and from the set every day. He didn't mind keeping the car windows down after he learned I was a Christian and enjoyed talking about God. I paid a couple visits to the church he and his wife attended, but the more I hung out with them, the more I realized they weren't my new family. When I mentioned techniques for resisting demonic attacks from Jezebel and dissolving religious structures, they simply stared at me oddly.

If Christians in a little southern town weren't willing to go that far, my costars certainly wouldn't. Aside from that, I'd been a professional actress long enough to understand that, while a Hollywood studio is a creative environment, it is also a workplace. Politics and religion were still taboo topics at work and dinner tables back then, because what we were producing was more important than everyone agreeing with us.

I did spoke openly about leaving town to visit family in Idaho. Until, that is, enough polite small conversation begins with "Where are you from, Joy?"" elicited a bewildered expression and the conclusion that whatever was in Idaho was not my true relatives at all.

"You live near your mother in Los Angeles and your father in New Jersey, but you spend all of your free time with a group in Idaho.""

I never knew how to answer. The response was yes, but the way they phrased it made it seem weird. How do I describe years of bonding, spiritual growth, and friendship to someone who has never experienced them? I determined early on that the less I said about my spiritual life, the better off I would be.

Keeping my inner life hidden just contributed to my loneliness. I wanted to join the actors and crew on all of their bonding experiences, but I was frightened of being "double-minded," as Les had said. How could I bond with them while keeping my deepest inner self hidden? I'd lie to everyone to obtain a false sense of belonging. I was afraid my lifelong craving for approval would take control and I'd lose all the spiritual ground I'd gained.

During my final visit to the Big House before departing for Wilmington, Les told me over a late-night chat on the front porch, "What happens is we become addicted to the high." The dopamine rush you experience from focusing on people you believe are outstanding is addictive. There is a part of you that wants something from the individuals you work with. So, you must treat yourself like an addict. Simply remove yourself from circumstances where you will be tempted.

To do this, I rented a property on Wrightsville Beach that was away from all the action. Instead of going out to drink with the cast and crew, I stayed at home and created songs on my piano, practiced my lines, and waited for visitors from my new family.

Emily was the first. She remained for a week to tour the set and meet everyone. She was affable and readily absorbed into the scene because, as a talent manager, she was already very familiar with Hollywood.

With the weather finally decreasing as the winter months neared, Emily and I went for long beach walks with tea and jackets. On our final stroll before she went, she informed me of a significant life shift.

"So, I have some exciting news! I am moving to Idaho!"

"Whoa, bury that lede!"

"I know—I didn't want to take away from celebrating you here, but I'm so excited."

"Have you gotten an apartment?"

"No, I'm gonna room with Jas for a few months until I find a place."

"Wait, are you going to quit your job?"

"I am!"

"Why? You've worked extremely hard to get where you are!"

"I've been chatting a lot with Les and Pam, and the problem is, I genuinely want to be a wife and mother, and staying in LA is only going to help my career. I want to take the leap of faith to show God that I'm ready for the next step—you know, to make room in my life for what's important to me. I can always return to work, but my time as a mother is limited. And I don't think I'll meet anyone in LA."

"I can't believe you're quitting this industry. That's crazy. I bet your biological mother will be very upset."

"Oh, yeah." She rolled her eyes and moaned. "The Jezebel spirit is strong. She genuinely attempted to whisk me off to some relatives in Sweden. The closer I get to the Lord, the more she flips out because she can no longer control me. She's angry at Pam because she feels betrayed. She was like, 'I've known Pam for twenty years and trusted her to look after you, and now she's got some crazy desire to make you her own daughter!' Like, she can't take the idea that God has provided me with a mother figure to fill in all the voids that she couldn't fill on her own."

I shook my head, knowing that my own mother felt the same way. The ocean breeze blew over us. "This stuff is not easy," I said. "I think of Camille and how she couldn't make room for the gift God was providing her by having Pam as her spiritual mother. The enemy will always want to hinder us from receiving God's gifts, but you won't let him. "I am proud of you."

"I'm so proud of you!" she stated. "It is difficult to be so far away from your entire neighborhood. And to remain firm and refuse to conform to the way everyone else lives their lives? You're inspirational!"

"Where are you going to work?""I asked her.

"Oh! I completely forgot to inform you. Les is buying a hotel to convert into a ministry center, and I will run it!"

"What?"I got thrown. How was Les going to afford a hotel? Everything in his and the Big House Family's lives was poor. He didn't have a job and was only beginning to plan his new ministry. I was unsure how they could afford anything.

"Howww...I mean..." I laughed nervously. "How?"

Emily obviously understood. She shrugged her shoulders and raised her hands. "He claims he has a plan!"

CHAPTER FIFTEEN

Since the talk about "spiritual authority" the previous summer, the group had began to more clearly differentiate who were the "children" and who were the "parents." Les and Martine, Pam and Ed, and Kurt and Lucy had established distinct roles as parents. In fact, they made it official by organizing a leadership council known as the Hamoatzah, which is Hebrew for "council."

The group's official nature necessitated further meetings among the six members. Les explained why he and Kurt were flying to meet me but just staying for one night. I trusted them, though I now feel they were aware that if they remained more than one night, I would urge they come to the set, and they didn't want to create any concerns by being introduced to my coworkers. Also, they just needed one night to ask me for money for the hotel—the true motive for their visit. That evening, we had burgers at the downtown Irish pub. Everyone else in the place was drinking Guinness. We stuck with sodas. They sat across from me, looking more presentable than normal. Collared shirts with combed hair. This was how they dressed up for a business meeting. Kurt handed me a foldout pamphlet that they had created and printed at Kinko's. The front featured a photo of a Quality Inn and Conference Center with the words "A DREAM COME TRUE." A PROPHECY WAS FULFILLED.

"Ohhh, it's a motel!" "I said." "Emily said it was a hotel." A motel still felt expensive, but it made more sense.

"Really?" Kurt asked. "We just flew all the way out here, and you're going to start this meeting by depreciating us? Okay, Hollywood."

My cheeks reddened. I was frightened of being misunderstood by those I adored the most. Not that I loved Kurt, but I didn't know how to deal with guys being angry with me—or anyone, really, with the exception of my parents—but males in particular. Kurt's temper often seemed to be on the verge of bursting.

I shake my head. "Sorry! That is not what I intended to do."

Les smiled. "No, it's okay," he said. "You've been put up in so many nice places all over the world with your acting jobs, I understand that hotels might look different to you than most people who haven't had that extreme privilege."

He was correct that I had stayed in many lovely locations, but I recognized the distinction between a hotel and a motel. I was not a complete moron. A hotel is where you stay with your family on vacation, whereas a motel is where you stay when picking up a hooker or driving a Mountain Dew truck across the country. Nevertheless, I did not want to argue. It didn't matter to me what they called it. It was their dream.

It is not a woman's responsibility to counsel or correct men. That was in the Jezebel book we'd all been studying.

Kurt let out a sharp exhale-laugh and got over his irritation. "We've been praying about a vision that kept showing up during Hamoatzah sessions. God has been able to provide so much healing at the Big House, and we want to share that on a broader scale."

"We see the massive potential for God to shake up this area by bringing our Family into one place where we can just love on people," he stated.

Keep loving. The way he said it was unusual. I figured he meant to let people know they're liked, which is a nice and natural thing to do. Right?

"We understand how much you enjoy hospitality. I mean, it's one of my and Marti's favorite things about you—the way you're always leaving small messages for people, arranging the bathroom washcloths exactly so, and making fresh flower arrangements. You have such a heart to make people feel seen and valued, and we believe this is a great fit for you."

"We have several investors so far," Kurt remarked. "Dontay's mom is giving sixty-five—"

"Seventy-five," Les corrected.

"Right, 75. And Ed and Pam, of course, are going for fifty."

"Thousand?" I expressed amazement.

"Yes," Kurt replied, unable to hide his annoyance for long. "And that's dollars, not pesos."

"It's a real family business," Les explained. "And with you here, so far away from everyone, this would be an excellent opportunity for you to remain involved. You know, you can help us paint the rooms and prepare the hospitality rollout for when visitors arrive. I believe you would have a lot of fun."

"Yeah, it does sound fun," I replied. It didn't actually. The main reason I enjoyed hospitality was to express affection to my loved ones. Doing it for complete strangers at a Quality Inn in Idaho was not my idea of fun, but I didn't say anything since I knew that one way I could show devotion to my loved ones was to support their aspirations.

"So, you're making what per episode on this show?" Les asked.

Money was never discussed in my family. Probably because there was none of it. And, as an actress, you never disclosed your income. Contract discussions were conducted in secret. I don't recall anyone asking me that question aside from my manager and the New York firm that handled my financial advice. But the silence was becoming uncomfortable, and I believed if this was a true Family, we should be able to communicate anything with one another.

"Um, forty-five, I believe? "Yes, something like that."

"Okay," I replied, "for you, maybe coming in at ten is a safe bet, because you're doing, what, twenty-two episodes?"

"If we don't get canceled," I said. "Which the producers always tell us we're about to be." We knew the show was growing in popularity, but because we lived in Wilmington before social media, we had no idea how well we were doing. I now believe this was intentional on the part of our show's creator and network executives—an attempt to discourage us from having inflated egos, becoming overly pushy, or, most importantly, gathering together to renegotiate our contracts collectively. They would inform us for the following eight seasons that "we're about to be canceled."

"But you have a guarantee of a certain amount of episodes in your contract, right?" Kurt asked. "I mean, we don't know anything about Hollywood, but Emily and Harker said that's kind of how it works."

"I can't remember what they landed on," I remarked. "Math and legal stuff scare me, so I just let my manager make the deals."

Les smiled. "Okay, 10 is a decent number. That's really nothing for you. The best part for you is that because it is a ministry initiative, it is tax deductible. And, really, it's a risk-free investment.

"We could easily do this with the bank," says Kurt, "but we just wanted to give you a chance to invest in and benefit from what God is doing."

Les arched his brow as he tilted his head to face me. "Wanna come in at ten?"

I felt so grown up negotiating agreements.

"Yeah!" I replied. "That sounds incredible!" But why is it for sale? Is something wrong with it?

Kurt became irritated yet again. "No, there is nothing wrong with it." You think we walked in here without doing any homework and are going to try to sell you a lemon?"

"No, I don't think that," I replied. "I'm just wondering why they're selling it."

"Do you not understand how loved you are?" Kurt asked him. "How protective are we of you?" Nobody wants to see you fail. We are on your side! "Do you not understand that?"

"Yeah, baby," Les replied. "There is nothing wrong with the hotel. Companies who own a large number of properties like this do exactly what they advertise. They always flip them. It's actually an excellent property. It's just off the freeway. There is a convention center linked to it, as shown here."

He turned the brochure over and pointed to a glossy image of a low gray stucco box in the middle of a parking lot.

"Think about all the ministries we could help out of this space," Les told us. "We could have church services there, do homeless outreach, host women's retreats and guest speakers."

His Welsh prophet friend had already agreed to be the first. It sounded like a fantastic way to contribute to the community, and I believed in amazing, magical things, such as someone with no hospitality industry expertise running a multimillion-dollar firm overnight.

Later that night, in bed, I read the brochure more carefully. Les and his first ministry were discussed in greater detail within. According to the text, the journey began with Christians praying for the Holy Spirit to come and dwell among them. The Holy Spirit appeared, and events began to unfold. Miracles started to become increasingly common. One man was healed after a documented incidence of congenital heart disease claimed the lives of his father and brother. His clear bill of health caused ripples of praise, followed by tremors of worry. The religious leaders got increasingly concerned, and they had to urge us to leave despite our wish to stay.

I was fascinated. First, I had never heard this story before, and second, I couldn't fathom somebody publishing a business booklet without spell-check. He was also throwing commas like confetti. What a disaster.

Do not be a snob, Joy. Everyone is good at different things.

Instead, I thought about how humble Les was that this incredible thing happened without bragging to any of us. He was just sharing it now as a proof of God's goodness. This guy spent six years in the marines teaching snipers, raised three boys, pastored a church in New York, then traveled across the nation to lead a charismatic movement of miracles in an Oregon church, got kicked out as a result, and was now starting anew!

I thought, "What an amazing person." I'd want to help him realize his dream. My aim was not to operate a hotel, but to facilitate a ministry that would aid others.

I called my New York-based financial advising business and expressed my desire to invest. They stated they felt it was a poor idea, but I knew they didn't see things through spiritual eyes as I did. God was going to do something great and surprise us all!

I directed them to cut the $10,000 check.

CHAPTER SIXTEEN

Over the next few months, I stayed up to date on happenings in Idaho via phone talks with Jasmine and Emily, as well as the Family's group email chain. Like this one from Les:

Dear Family,

Update from this Wednesday Family meeting: What a privilege it was, for us to welcome Harker & Mina's precious little girl into our Family. Now as she is pregnant again we have the extrordinary honor to flood Mina with prayers during this time when the enemy would seek to discourage her with lies about her identity because post-pardum is not from God.

Dontay, is also asking for your prayers in his new role in Maintenance at the Hotel! We give glory to God for the miraculous way our Savior has turned Dontay's life around and now, he is able to do his own ministry through serving our guests. We're just blown away by this man of God who walked away from the worldly temptations he was offered in sports, in order to serve behind the scenes. He is making himself lowly, like Jesus, and I'm humbled that he calls me "Papa." I'm proud of you, my boy. You are famous in heaven!

Please also continue to pray for our beautiful Joy, braving the beasts of Hollywood in North Carolina. Joy, you are not alone! We are all here behind you holding you up, in prayer.

We Are a Ship!

Les

I appreciated the emails and phone calls, but we were living quite different lifestyles. My hours were long, and when I wasn't working on the program, I would write music, paint, sew, or do anything creative. I was still the kid who played in Grandma Doris' attic and loved my own company. By the time winter hit, I didn't feel as connected to everyone as I once did. I was feeling quite alone again, just like I had before the group.

I enjoyed the early-morning call times; I loved unfurling myself onto the hair chair and cackling with the Mama Bears; I loved coming onto set, running lines in an oversized puffy coat with half my makeup done and my hair in gigantic Velcro rollers; and I loved having so much creative freedom. That was the most significant distinction between being one of a show's stars and appearing as a guest star on another show. As a guest star, I always followed the director's ideas. Now I felt comfortable and encouraged to add my own.

Unfortunately, because I had ADHD and OCD, which were not diagnosed until years later, I occasionally overreacted. I'd dwell on something unimportant to everyone else, like a newly cooked pie on the counter in my character's kitchen. Everyone else used set decoration, but I couldn't move forward in a scenario unless I knew why the pie was there.

"I'd love to have you start over by the window and end the phone call over here by the kitchen counter," the director would say.

"Okay, no problem. However, have you noticed this pie on the counter?"

"The pie?" Um, yes, it is in the shot."

"I'm just wondering when Haley would have had the time to bake a pie today if she's been running all over town."

"Uh, okay. "She brought it home from Karen's Café.

"Okay. But, who is it for? I'm just alone on the phone in this moment, I don't have any scenes eating pie later, and I'm not at home for the remainder of the episode."

Confused, the director would propose: "Haven't you ever just brought home a dessert for yourself?"

"Yes, but this one is uncovered on the counter, steaming."

"I only want some movement in the backdrop. "The steam looks nice in the light."

"Totally. "Except, never mind."

"What?"

"Well, the steam implies either I just baked it, which we know I didn't, or that I just heated it up because I plan to eat it right now, which we also know isn't happening because Haley is about to leave again."

The director would exclaim, frustrated, "Set Dec? "Can we lose the pie?"

"Unless you want to cut the pie and I can eat a slice during the phone call," I would respond. "I think I could make that make sense."

"Do you want to eat pie during the phone call?"

"I mean, I don't think it's really a pie-eating kind of call, but if you need it for the shot…"

"We only have one pie," the set decorator would announce, "so we can't reset it."

"Okay, no pie," the director would respond. "Just lose the pie."

"I'm sorry; I just want it to make sense." "I am sorry."

What I didn't realize at the time was that I had been surrendering myself in tiny increments with Les, to the point where I was instinctively clutching for control in whatever manner I could, like fighting over pie.

I attempted to keep these spirals to a minimal, especially after hearing comments from producers via my manager: "Joy's so talented, but... difficult." My manager told me not to worry about it because she didn't like the show's producers or creator. We were in our early twenties, and none of us had ever been series regulars on a network TV show, so we had no idea what to expect. Several times, I walked into the wardrobe and found ten bras put out for me to try on, be photographed in, and have the images sent back to the producers so they could choose one.

"Oh, I don't really want to be in a bra on TV," I'd say. "I don't think it suits my character much, it's not in the script, and it has nothing to do with the scene, anyway."

"This is what the creator wants you to wear in the scene," the wardrobe designer would explain, apologizing.

When I stayed firm on religious modesty, my manager would call and say, "She is being difficult again. "We told you what the show was about!"

In all honesty, they did. The "fucking and sucking" executive had been very clear about this. I guess I just looked at my persona and assumed that was other people's narratives. There was no nudity clause in my contract requiring me to strip down to my underwear on television. But my manager was in LA, three hours behind North Carolina, so every time I tried to contact her to explain the situation and beg her to intercede, it slowed down production, making me appear even more "difficult" to everyone else. Now I understand the parallels between the creator's strategy and Les' strategy. In retrospect, it was evident that they both utilized geography to separate us young and trusting people from our support networks and to drive us into doing what they wanted.

However, whereas the creator's sole leverage was fame, Les' leverage was my eternal salvation. The decision was easy. And Les had been teaching us that worldly opposition was a sign from God, citing 2 Timothy 3:12: "Everyone who wants to live a godly life in Christ Jesus will be persecuted." The more my personal values and preferences clashed with the creator's demands, the more he began inserting elements into the tales that I think were intended to humiliate or anger me. Like making other characters refer to Haley as "fat." Or having Haley "overreact" when her high school boyfriend watches pornography. That was a huge battle. I felt the dialogue created for Haley as humiliating and disrespectful to the young ladies who looked up to me. I tried talking to the creator about it, but by the day of filming, not much had changed, so I rewrote a lot of my own lines for that episode. It confused and irritated the director, other performers, script supervisor, and producers, and I felt terrible. But I wasn't sure what else to do. It consistently came down to valuing myself and my convictions versus giving up and saying, "Ugh, it's not worth the fight." And I had trained myself to stick to my principles no matter what the cost.

Despite Les and Pam's insistence that no one in Wilmington was "spiritually safe" for me to trust, I began to enjoy the company of my costars.
I spent more and more time outside of my trailer, frequently watching Chad, James, and other cast and crew members play basketball in between sets. James' collaboration with the basketball coordinator had truly paid off. He was already a good athlete, but learning from a true professional gave him an advantage that made filming the basketball scenes easier, and they were more fascinating to watch since we knew it was James, not a stunt actor, doing the majority of these remarkable moves. James was also quite private on set. In between setups, his nose was frequently buried in great literature like Moby Dick or Kerouac, while I was knitting or drafting a script on my laptop from my cast chair. We didn't mingle much outside of work, but on screen we were creating a heavy-hitting love story, which felt hilarious given how stagnant my personal dating life was. Paul Johansson and Craig Sheffer were the two men that filled the lack of male companionship, and I could often find them over dinner ordering expensive wine and arguing religion or discussing art and philosophy for hours.
Tired of the loneliness of my beach home rental, I relocated downtown to be closer to the action and become a more active member of this new community. I discovered a creaky—or what the ad termed as "historic"—home on Orange Street. I adorned it with huge velvet drapes and antique finds such as elaborate side tables, a pink brocade fainting sofa, and a mannequin dress form.
For the first time since leaving New York, I began to feel like myself. And then one night, Les called. He always seemed to know

when any of us were becoming aloof or intrigued about life beyond the Family. He could know how I was feeling from almost two thousand miles away. He grew irritated when he discovered I had left the beach home.

"Did you tell anyone before you did that?" the man inquired.

"I didn't realize I needed to ask anyone before I moved," I claimed. "It simply seemed like a nice idea. I felt too lonely out there."

He paused and sighed. "That's the entire purpose, baby. It is not beneficial for you to do things alone. That's simply an old way of life for you. It's fine to seek for assistance. Lean on your family; we are here for you.

"Yes, I understand that. And thank you. I didn't think where I lived mattered to anyone."

"Everything you do matters. "We care about you!" He hesitated again, and I sat in displeasure with myself. "You know, it might be worth having a meeting about this when you're back here for Christmas."

I had already sent an email to the group informing them that I would be spending another Christmas with them, despite my mother's best efforts to persuade me to spend it with her.

"What do you mean, 'a meeting'?" I inquired.

"Well, you've been trying to do everything on your own. I mean, throughout your entire life. Your parents had a lot to worry about, and you've been raising yourself all these years."

That was true, I knew. But as he mentioned them, I realized how much I was beginning to miss my parents. My father was still in New Jersey, but he lived in a new house with his wife and my younger brother, whom I knew little about. Early in my time in Los Angeles, I had begun to develop positive ties with my stepfather and his two daughters, but we hadn't spoken in about a year. Perhaps I missed the life I previously had rather than them. Grandma and the attic; Blue Eyes and the lake—a life that no longer existed. I felt completely disoriented, and Idaho was the only place I felt I truly belonged.

"Joy, let's have a family meeting where you can share your struggles. Everyone may listen and offer truth to you in places where you are discouraged."

"Like a meeting with the entire Family, and everyone just has to sit there and listen to my problems?"

"Not, 'has to.' We get to. It is a privilege to press into each other, and you are providing us the opportunity to improve our ability to hear from God, understand true sacrifice, and love you. That is what families do. I know you didn't have that growing up, but family meetings are very common."

I was quiet. I hadn't considered it that way before.

"You obviously don't have to if you're not comfortable or don't trust everyone here."

"Oh, no, I totally trust everybody," I replied. "I suppose it feels selfish to want a large bunch of people to sit around and listen to me gripe. I have a wonderful life. My issues pale in comparison to those of many others."

"But don't you feel blessed when one of your sisters here calls you to ask for advice or prayer?"

"Yeah."

"How is this different? Do not withhold a blessing for others out of pride. Pride comes before the fall, correct? Proverbs 16:18. You have the opportunity to be a big benefit in everyone's life here simply by sharing your heart.

I listened. I wanted nothing more than to have a purpose. If all it needed to make a difference in the lives of the individuals I had grown to love was to let go of my ego and embarrassment and share my heart, I would do it.

"Yes, that makes sense," I replied.

"Good," Les remarked. "I'll set it up."

CHAPTER SEVENTEEN

Les began holding twice-monthly church services in the conference center as soon as the motel acquisition was completed. Unlike the Wednesday night gatherings at the Big House, they were open to the general public. Dontay was the family member most knowledgeable with computers, so he created a website. However, these were rarely updated with dates and times, thus the people who went were members of the Big House Family, as well as friends and extended bio-family. Emily's father, who came over on occasion at Emily's invitation and was always glad to see Ed and Pam, but was plainly not a fan of Les and avoided him; Miguel and Juana's cousins; some of Lucy's Mary Kay pals; Kurt's brother, who was even stranger than him. Because meeting hours were vague, folks relied on Les to announce dates (typically at the last minute) to Big House Family members, and we were responsible for informing anyone we wanted to invite. It was simply a means of managing everyone's intentions. You never know when the next service will be, so stop everything when it happens!

Similarly, there was mayhem in the motel.

"There's so much renovating that needs to be done," Dontay informed me. He was in charge of maintenance, despite having only ever used his hands to catch a football. Things shatter every day. But I am learning a lot! I just learned how to fix a hotel ice machine. I never knew how to do it before!"

Emily had even more obstacles as the motel's manager—a position she was given because her former job also included the word "manager" in the title.

"Honestly, every time I make a decision about anything, it seems to be wrong," she told me. "If I don't run everything by Les or Kurt, then there's always a problem." There was an issue yesterday regarding how the towels should be folded. I had requested the staff to do this double foldover thing—I did some research—and they were doing it nicely, but Les suggested that instead of hanging longways, they be folded to seem puffier and more square. They summoned me for an hour-long meeting about working too independently. Kurt also gave me a speech about presentation, hospitality, and how the staff should and should not use their time. Apparently, my method of folding towels takes twice as long, which I do not believe is true. But they are currently asking me to consult with them on absolutely everything. So it's just difficult to get anything done. Even if it's unpleasant, the truth is that I don't want to be running around on my own, making decisions that are contrary to God's vision for this area. So it's probably beneficial for me."

Les and Pam, together with other leaders, had effectively trained, conditioned, and groomed us. As soon as we started moaning, no matter how justified, we stopped ourselves, punished ourselves for being so negative, spoiled, and ungrateful, and converted it into a blessing—an chance for learning and progress.

Even yet, it was difficult to put a positive spin on the motel when I eventually saw it in person during Christmas. What a piece of trash. Old carpet. Poor fluorescent lighting. The proximity to the freeway resulted in never-ending smog and a steady stream of shady drifters lingering in the parking lot.

The Big House was not in much better condition. When I came in, I saw many heaps of dried cat feces in the formal dining room. Perhaps it was vomit. Whatever it was, it had been there for a long time, accompanied with several yellow stains. The entire foyer smelled like Salami's litter box. When I pointed it out to Dontay, he responded, "Oh man, Pop keeps telling me to clean that up, but I keep forgetting." Ugh, I get so tired of staying at the motel every day.

"Isn't she... his cat?"

"Yeah, but I told him I would do it, so he's just waiting until I follow through."

"What is Pam's opinion on all of this? I mean, her magnificent house is being ripped down."

"I understand. I feel awful about it. But, I believe Jas asked her about it the other day, and she said we needed to show grace for Les and the boys. Nobody is perfect, so we should simply speak the truth about them and let the Lord to help them improve their habits."

"The truth being...?" I asked.

"You know, 'You're so good at keeping the house clean,' 'You're great stewards of this house,' like that."

It was the same advice Les had offered Emily years ago in LA concerning her brother's negative attitude—a strategy we'd all been attempting to execute in different ways. As I glanced at the piles of cat excrement, it didn't appear to be working.

Walking into the back bedroom, I discovered Gretchen's bed was even messier than before: tissues, hair ties, crumpled garments and balled-up dirty socks, wrappers, and an empty Coke can. Jasmine's side was still clean and organized. It was similar to the episode of I Love Lucy where Lucy partitions off the living room because she is weary of Ricky making a mess.

Even more concerning was the big hole in QB's bedroom door. Apparently, one of the Barbarians had enraged him, and QB punched right through the door. He was now walking about with a thick brace on his wrist and torn knuckles. Given how frequently Les mentioned war and warriors, this level of aggressiveness was unsurprising. He stated the enemy was assaulting our family and bemoaned how males had grown weak and allowed women to walk all over them. "Men were built for war!" he frequently exclaimed, before telling us anecdotes about his time in the marines. This appeared to be represented in a couple of new decorations in the house: in the living room, there was now a large oil painting print of a man-of-war at sea. He was following his vision's nautical theme—under a magnet on the fridge was a piece of paper with the words WE ARE A SHIP written in large letters. I was relieved that there were no mistakes in the motel brochure.

Les thought QB's assault on the door was humorous, and jokingly mentioned it in an email to the group, so I attempted to laugh it off too. I did not grow up with brothers. Maybe it's just what boys do. I wondered how Pam and Ed felt about seeing their stately mansion deteriorate. We hadn't entered Grey Gardens territory yet, but they couldn't have been pleased. Pam isn't hand-sanitizer-ready, and she's eating from the restroom floor. How could she have been comfortable with this?

Again, reflexively, I quickly blamed myself for being so judgmental about the condition of the house. You're so snobby from living in your big, beautiful, old southern palace with its gorgeous curtains and antique furniture doing some silly TV show while these people here are devoting their lives to God and aren't concerned with material things. It's none of your business how Pam is dealing with it. That's between her and God. Maybe it's good for her to not be so neurotic!

Dontay's mother was not brainwashed; she had come to spend Christmas with her son and his "new family"—as well as to check on her investment in the motel as the greatest sponsor. Her name was Esther John Valentine, which I was relieved to learn since she had such a dazzling presence that hearing her say anything like "Hello, I'm Janet" would have been a huge disappointment. When I met her, I thought of bumblebees. The defiance of physics they enjoy by flying with a carriage too huge for their wings was reminiscent of Esther's bafflingly large breasts dangling waistless over bamboo-thin legs. I spent a lot of time over the holidays figuring out which muscles in her body worked the hardest to keep her upright.

Esther was not as wary of the group as my parents and Emily's parents were. She had never met Les, but they exchanged cordial emails on a daily basis, and he provided her links to his weekly sermons. With church held in the conference center twice a month—or whenever he felt like preaching—Les recorded his sermons and had Dontay upload them on YouTube.

Esther was thrilled to learn how much Dontay contributed to the ministry. She was also thrilled to find that he had gotten engaged. Another reason she came for the trip was to meet her soon-to-be daughter-in-law, Jasmine.

Jasmine called to inform me a few weeks before the holiday. Of course, I was pleased for her. But I was also slightly disappointed. Not because I had feelings for Dontay; my crush on him had faded. I realized I loved him like a brother, and I knew that when I married, I wanted passionate attraction, sparks, and chemistry. I was just running out of options. Most of the boys on One Tree Hill were in relationships, and they weren't Christians, so they were off-limits anyhow. But I despised being a lively young lady in her twenties and seeing everyone around me pair off. Sophia and Hilarie were in romances, Paul was always involved with someone, and recurring actors were coming into town and forming little "locationships." Now that Mina was with Harker and Jasmine was with Dontay, Abe and QB were the only unmarried boys left in the family. Which basically meant simply Abe, because I had no interest in QB—even before the door was destroyed.

Esther was pleased to meet Jasmine. They hit it off immediately away. But a few hours later, her entire manner transformed. Because during that time, she had gone to the motel with Les. When she returned through the front entrance, she appeared to have changed. Her energy level was low, and she appeared to be glancing around the home warily. Dontay had put her suitcase in Ed and Pam's garage apartment, where she intended to spend the night. She retreated into their space for approximately five minutes before reappearing with her bag, passing by the guest room, where Emily and I were stooped over, crafting on the floor.

"Esther, where are you going?""I asked. "I thought you were staying here."

"Well, I did, too, but I guess there was a mix-up, so I'll be staying at a hotel instead."

"Our hotel?""

Esther snorted derisively. "It's a motel," she explained. "It's barely even that. No, I'll be staying somewhere else." She then took a long look at me. "Where is your family, dear?"

"Um, my mom's in California and my dad's in New Jersey." Given Esther's attitude, and not wanting to insult her as a parent, I avoided using the terms "bio-mom" and "bio-dad."

"Are you close to them?""
"Not really." I mean, I adore them; they're lovely people. But I feel more at home here. "It feels more like family to me."
She nodded, staring at me for slightly longer than was comfortable.
"Well, I am delighted you got to view the motel. It was a large investment for me as well. "I'm excited about the ministry's vision."
"Did you invest?"
I nodded.
"How much, if you do not mind my asking?"
"Um, ten."
Her entire forehead muscles tensed up. "Really?"
"It's okay," I answered, sensing her apprehension. "I have a weird job that pays me well."
"Well, I'm sure you have good financial advisers then and you know what you're doing."
I thought about my financial experts, who were completely opposed to this investment.
Esther nodded to herself and moved on to the door.
"See you tomorrow at Christmas," I promised.
She looked back at me and said, "Goodbye, dear."

Christmas morning, jet-lagged and still on Eastern Time, I awoke to a gloomy house. I strolled quietly toward the kitchen to prepare coffee, but I heard low conversations in the living room. I paused and listened.
"He just contradicts everything that I say," Les replied gently. "It's like he's actively trying to create division in our Family."
That would have been the time for me to make my presence known in some way. Coughing, turning on a light, or even moving around the kitchen. Except, I really wanted to know what was going on.
Next, I heard Kurt's voice. "Everyone is only loyal to him because he is so amazing. "He's smart and attractive—"
"And he knows it."
"He knows it. Right. Initially, they were pals with many of these guys.
"So his views will be taken seriously since people trust him. "And Mina."
"And Mina." Right. Kurt added, "But she's not very credible right now with the whole postpartum thing." "I'm not too worried about

her."

"I know we're calling it postpartum," Les explained. "But, honestly?"

"I think she is bipolar."

"Might be."

"The tricky aspect is that we're still in the early stages, you know? Harker's actions may disrupt God's plan.

"Yes, that level of independence can allow the enemy to gain a foothold. "If he starts openly discussing his thoughts that directly contradict the Hamoatzah..."

There was quiet. I inhaled quietly as possible. My body was beginning to itch from being frozen in place, should a cracking floorboard reveal my trespass.

"Where is Pam with all of this?Kurt asked.

"I think she's with us," Les remarked. "She obviously loves her son, but she doesn't want to cause misunderstanding. And all the girls look up to her."

"Well, that's why I asked."

They halted again, and I could hear them shifting places on the furniture. It truly was that black. Why are they just sitting in the darkness?

"Well, I'm glad we're on the same page," Kurt responded. "It's critical that we project a consistent, you know, presence as leaders. So let's just talk to him and clarify—"

"I'll talk with him," Les said.

"All right, well, sooner than later."

"I'll do it when the time is right," Les replied forcefully. "Don't forget there's only one reason you're here."

What does this mean? I wondered.

Then they began to move away from the furniture, with footsteps leading somewhere. Every room in this house appeared to be connected to two others, so anyone could appear unexpectedly from any direction. I began gently walking backward, hoping the floor would not creak, but I didn't get far before hearing Kurt unlock and close the cellar door.

Okay, he is gone. One down.

However, Les's footsteps continued to move. I was unsure which path to go. He could be heading directly toward me or back to his room.

You are an actress. Act! I began humming. Better to be captured on

my own terms. I walked confidently into the kitchen, and there he was, turning the corner at the same time as me.
"Oh!"I pretended to be startled. "Morning!"I am a lousy liar. Good actress, poor liar.
"Hey, baby." His voice rose two decibels. "You're up early."
"The time change…"
"Well, Merry Christmas." He hugged me.
"Merry Christmas!"" I was generally reassured by Les' hugs, but after overhearing that talk and lying to him right then, I became uneasy.
"You been awake for a while?He asked.
"I just rolled out of bed. Coffee."
"I came down to make some, too."
It was the slowest coffee I'd ever waited for. I wasn't often alone with Les—there were always too many people and too much commotion—and under normal circumstances, I would have been thrilled to spend one-on-one time with him. These were not ordinary conditions. I tried to seem upbeat as we discussed Christmas presents and plans for the day. Finally, the coffee was ready. I brought mine back into the dark bedroom and turned on a book light. I attempted to read my Bible while I waited for Jasmine or Gretchen to wake up, but I couldn't stop thinking about what I had heard. Could Mina actually be bipolar? What exactly was Harker attempting to "derail," and why? I detest that my suspicion fell on them rather than Les and Kurt's clear, malicious scheming.

A few hours later, we met in the living room for a DIY Secret Santa exchange. This year, I got Martine. I decided to make her a silk robe and hired a private sewing tutor from Wilmington to teach me how. It came out beautifully, and I couldn't wait to give it to her.
Les began the present exchange with a prayer, followed by one of his regular monologues. "Look at us, we managed to gather everyone in one room for Christmas again!"
I looked around and didn't see Esther. I said to Dontay across the room, "Where is your mother?"
He shakes his head. He said, "Not coming."
Why?
He was ready to respond, but Les was still speaking, so Dontay waved me off: "Tell you later."

"Thank you, everyone, for the sacrifice you're making by choosing to celebrate with your spiritual Family instead of your bio-families this year," he said. "I understand that it is not always easy to do, especially given the expectations that many families have of one another." It takes guts to do things God's way even when others tell you it doesn't make sense. Jesus frequently performed things that confused the Pharisees and even his own disciples. The Lord's method appears silly to the world, but everyone in this room has chosen to—well, look dumb! All for the sake of fulfilling God's calling on your life. So just lend a help!"

Everyone applauded, but I noted Harker was reluctant to join and quick to go, which appeared to reinforce the disagreement I'd heard Les and Kurt discussing. Harker's failure to clap more passionately made me see him as the underminer rather than the undermined.

"I am so proud of the safe space we've created for each other," she said. He then motioned to Dontay. "I understand that was difficult for you, son, therefore I appreciate you setting that barrier and making that sacrifice. If someone in the room wasn't a member of this spiritual Family, the vulnerability that God is bringing us into today may be unpleasant."

"I gotchu, Pop," Dontay said. "It's completely worth it." We must have that level of safety."

That should do it, I thought. And it felt safe. We enjoyed a little worship period before exchanging gifts. As everyone stood up to get a snack or refill their drink, Les approached me. His plump fingers were trapped inside the narrow handle of a coffee mug labeled I LIKE IT WHEN THEY CALL ME BIG POPPA.

"Would you please pray for Dontay?""He spoke quietly. "He's having trouble negotiating things with his mother. Esther's desire to control Dontay's life is heightened by his decision to choose his own family, triggering her Jezebel-like tendencies. You understand what that's like. I know your mother is also having difficulty accepting you as a member of this family."

"Oof. Yes. "Talk about control."

"It is frequent among so many women. Was your grandmother particularly controlling?"

"My mom's mother, yes!"I said. Unlike Doris, Nanny Marge was an Irish spark plug. If you angered her, she would save it in her pocket for a rainy day. She'd had a rich childhood until Black Tuesday,

1929, when she worked her way back to financial stability and had four children with a charming soldier who had a knack for betting on the wrong races. After losing everything to the railroad (and tossing a few cast-iron pots at him), she rebuilt and finally became a missionary in Papua New Guinea. By the time I was a child, she had returned to the United States and, because she believed her trials had earned her the right, she had something to say about everything in everyone's life. I adored her, admiring her abilities as a storyteller and armchair theologian. However, other family members found her annoying and cut her off completely.

"Jezebel is a generational spirit," he explained. "I'm proud of you for breaking the cycle and standing up to her."

Les took a sip from his coffee.

"She sent me an email," he explained. "Have I told you?"

"Who? My mom?"

"Yeah, she was asking questions about our theology as a church."

"She's always digging around in my life."

"Oh, she was lovely about it. I like your mom. I believe she is simply struggling to accept your decision to prioritize spiritual family over biological family. Would you like to read it?"

"I don't believe so, actually. "It will just irritate me."

He laughed. "Well, I don't mind chatting to her. So, if she ever bothers you about something, feel free to forward her to me. Your father, too. He's been a little more aggressive than your mother, so I'd be proud to protect you in all of that."

"My father?" What did he do?"

"Oh, I assumed you knew. He's been contacting members of my old church to find out more about me."

"Very bothersome. "I am sorry."

"Like I said, it's really common for bio-families to feel threatened when they realize they can't provide something that someone else can."

Why couldn't my parents just let me to be happy?

"Thanks so much for fielding all that, Les," I apologized.

"No problem, kiddo." He grinned and patted the side of my cheek with his palm. "We can discuss more of your personal matters in your meeting with the group tomorrow!""

"I look forward to it!"I said. I was not. I dreaded it. Despite discovering how run-down the motel was, seeing the growing filth at

the Big House, the perplexing encounter with Esther, and the enigmatic chat in the dark, I continued to believe in Les and our Big House Family. I remained optimistic that I would emerge from this imminent basement encounter with more clarity, faith, and healing.
"Oh!" Les said before exiting the room. "You keep a journal, right?"
"Yes, all the time!""
"Bring your most recent journal to the meeting." I think it could be useful."

I stepped slowly down the stained carpeted stairs to Kurt and Lucy's basement living quarters, where we girls still had to shower. I despised this basement. It was gloomy, uncomfortable, and went against all of my hospitality instincts. The walls were an unattractive brown. There were no plants. It was even drabber than the motel.
These meetings were common; I simply hadn't been here to witness them. That's it, I told myself. You have nothing to be concerned about.
When I reached the bottom of the stairs, I noticed that the lights were even weaker than usual. Pam, no doubt, had lighted a few candles to create a pleasant, inviting atmosphere, and the family was seated on sofas and chairs arranged in a semicircle. It did not feel homey; rather, it felt ritualistic.
Emily stood up and hugged me, rubbing my back while I gazed at the folding chair positioned in the center of the room. That'd be my seat until we were finished.
"Thank you for allowing us to do this!"She grinned.
I did notice a few people missing, however. QB, the Barbarians, and Brandon were never there at these sessions; they were too young to be of any spiritual "use," I suppose. However, Mina, Harker, Dontay, Miguel, Juana, and Lucy were missing.
"Should we wait for everybody else?"I asked.
Les was clear. "This is your group for today. Everyone here has been hand-picked—prayerfully chosen—for this meeting." He stated it like a chef assuring me that each of the twenty-five meals I'm going to have has been tailored to my precise taste preferences.
"Well, Lord," he said, "we come to you in Jesus' name, and we thank you. We are grateful for your immense love for us. And now we bring your loving daughter Joy before you in prayer, asking you to heal her. That her identity would no longer be defined by her

employment, but by who you say she is, who you created her to be as a child in your Heavenly home. Amen."

"Amen," we all echoed.

"So," Les said, "Joy was telling me about her self-esteem issues at work. There are certain childhood wounds and places in her that feel broken. We've all experienced the feeling of knowing we're faulty yet lack the means to repair it. So, Joy, why don't you just tell everyone the lay of the land in your heart right now, and then we can begin sowing into you?"

I swallowed. "Okay, well, thank you guys for taking the time out of your Friday night to come talk with me about this stuff and pray for me."

I realized I wasn't sure why I was even here. I did not call the meeting. I wasn't even sure what I had done wrong.

"I guess my heart is in a fairly good place, actually. I am finally starting to love my life in Wilmington. I don't feel so lonely anymore. I'm becoming increasingly creative in a variety of ways. I'm making friends, so why am I here? Find the problem, Joy. What is the problem? "I believe the problem is that the more comfortable I become there, the further away I feel from you all here, and you know, you're my family! So, I do not want it to happen.

I paused and looked around nervously, not knowing what else to say.

"We do not want that to happen, either!" Emily said, cheerfully and optimistically.

Gretchen added, "You're really important to us, sis." But she said it the same way she said everything else: with an over-the-top fervor that played on her desire to be useful. I chastised myself again for being critical.

"Joy, is this your journal?" Les inquired, referring to the hardcover book I had placed under my chair.

"Uh, yep."

"Could you please open that up for us and share anything you've written in the past few days?"

The only appropriate response was "Sure," but I did not want to do this. My journals were filled with my deepest, strangest, and most foolish thoughts—just a way to get them out of my system. I used to change my mind about something as soon as I saw it on paper. It was going to be excruciating. Is this what happens in all of these meetings? I opened my journal and searched for something meaningful but not too embarrassing.

"Okay, um, here's one." I read aloud: "'Lord, I'm frustrated with music right now. I have a lot of creative energy, yet I can't seem to finish anything. I want to sing and record an album, maybe even write a musical, but I don't know how to do all of the technical stuff to make it happen. Ugh, Joy, you're so lazy. Just learn how! At the very least, I am inspired! Last year, I felt so—BLAH, but today, in Wilmington, surrounded by artists, I feel like I'm regaining my strength. God, help me how to encourage others to feel your love. Like Sophia. To be honest, I'm terrified she'll reject me (and then you, God, because I didn't set a good example!), so I don't even approach her. It is so foolish! Please show me how to love her as you do! Hilarie and I are similar, which makes it easy for me to have fun with her.

"That's fantastic," Les replied, interrupting me mid-sentence. "You don't have to read the whole thing."

"Oh, okay."

"Does anyone sense anything from the Holy Spirit about that?" Les replied, giving Pam a sharp look and a nod.

"You're so precious, Joy," Pam added. "I absolutely adore hearing your feelings for your co-stars. "You're a devoted daughter and friend."

"Thanks."

"But, well, I couldn't help but notice how much self-focus there is in that entry. But perhaps it is just the one. I do not know. Are most of your entries like this?"

I rapidly looked through the journal. "I suppose so. But, well, it's my journal. Isn't that what a journal is? Myself?" I chuckled, but no one joined me.

"I would just say that perhaps the reason you're feeling more distant from your Family here at home is that you're filling up your thought life with yourself, rather than with God and others."

"Taking our thoughts captive is a very real, vital thing," says Les. "Paul teaches in 2 Corinthians 10 that we must be careful with what we allow into our brains. So, if you focus on your professional goals rather than believing that God would open those doors at the appropriate moment, you will be constantly rebellious, attempting to make things happen on your own. If you focus on how you behave with others rather than believing that God will just appear in the midst of your relationships, you are once again attempting to play God. Both of these things will separate you from the individuals who are here to help you stay on track: your family."

I attempted to follow his train of thought, but the more he said, the less I understood. I assumed it was because I had been in Wilmington and away from the family for a time. For example, I excelled in French during my tour to Paris but would now embarrass myself if I returned.

"You're letting yourself ask too many illegal questions," he told you.

"'Illegal questions'?"

"Thoughts you can no longer allow in, like wondering if you belong in this Family."

Had I questioned that? I did not think so.

Kurt then began discussing contracts, King David pledging fealty to the elders of Israel, and other allusions I was unfamiliar with, but they all related to my independence and rebellion.

Then Gretchen jumped in: "It's so easy to slip into double-mindedness, sis, but we're not gonna let you."

I found it difficult to take seriously coming from a Cheetos junkie who has no idea how to make her bed.

"What was that?"Les pounced on me."

"What?"

"That thought you just had when Gretchen spoke."

"Sorry—nothing. I—"

He pressed. "Not anything. What was it?"

"I thought that was hypocritical of her to say. "I am sorry, Gretch, but I do."

"But everyone is a hypocrite, Joy, including you. "You say you want to be a good friend, but you haven't come home to visit in a few months," Les explained.

"Well, the last few episodes have been a heavy storyline for Haley."

"But you've never had a problem coming home before, so... I'm sorry, but I'm only hearing excuses." And I'm not trying to hurt you, darling, but I find it quite convenient that when you're experiencing early success, you're also unable to make time for the individuals you know will keep you accountable. "I'm not buying it."

I remained nothing, and Gretchen spoke out again: "Yes, we are all hypocrites in different ways. "Family is made up of imperfect people, but that doesn't mean we don't support each other."

Then Kurt said, "This is the necessity of having a covenant connection with each other. We will not allow you get away with this, Joy. "You must stop believing lies about yourself."

Everything was said to me in a pleasant tone, with passion and intention. Les had devised a strategy to persuade everyone in the room, including me, that they were being kind by revealing and dissecting my old emotional wounds and linking them to current behaviors.

This lasted for three hours. There were restroom breaks, snack breaks, further journal reads, and dissections. The aim of the entire meeting was for me to confront my demons and "wrestle through."

Why are you still crying, baby girl?"Les inquired near the end.

"I feel like there's so much I'm doing wrong and I can never keep up."

Pam approached me and petted my knee. "Sweetheart, that is precisely the point. We can never meet all of God's requirements for perfection."

Jasmine whispered softly, "That's why we need Jes—" but Les interrupted her.

"That's why we need one another. We are aboard this ship together. We will not let you fall away. We're never going to let you go, no matter what happens on One Tree Hill or in your profession."

By the end of my meeting, everyone was exhausted and went to bed. I stayed up for a little longer, and despite my exhaustion, I was appreciative for everything this Family was willing to spend in me. Curled up in my beloved beanbag chair, I felt like I was under a spell. The Pacific Northwest possessed a distinct magic. North Carolina felt haunted from the ground up, as if unfinished stories were trying to emerge from beneath the dirt. But Idaho felt heavy in the air, with thick mist—not rising hot from the ocean, but weighing down cool from above. The wind behaved differently here. The secrets weren't in the graveyards; instead, they slithered through the tops of the trees, seeking refuge from the never-ending rain that felt like it was working with God to wash away everything old. That's all I needed. A continual cleaning. I opened my journal and wrote and wrote till my wrist ached. I had to write down everything I had just learnt so I wouldn't forget the truth. I was very fast to forget the reality about myself.

CHAPTER EIGHTEEN

"What in the world is all the commotion?" I inquired, peering out the window of the limo. "What, is Britney here, too?"

Hilarie, Sophia, Chad, James, and I were on our way to an appearance on MTV's Total Request Live in Times Square. But as we reached a block away from the studio, traffic came to a halt—the result of hundreds of students brandishing signs and spilling into the street.

"Oh my god, I think that's for us." Sophia laughed, astonished.

I looked closer at the signs.

Haley & Nathan 4 EVA!
Marry Me Chad!
OTH is my HOME

"Well, I guess people are watching the show," James observed with his usual dry humor.

The show had been renewed for more episodes and moved to a better time slot, so we knew we were growing a following, and in Wilmington, we'd started getting signature requests when we were downtown. However, the TRL mayhem made it evident that the show had become a full-fledged pop culture phenomenon. I didn't watch much TV growing up, but even I got caught up in the 90210 frenzy. Standing at the enormous window overlooking Broadway, peering down at the mob of shouting fans, with another crowd of screaming fans inside the studio, I couldn't believe this was happening to us. I was so nervous throughout the interview that my brain short-circuited. When host Damien Fahey asked me what it was like to work on the show, I rambled for a few seconds before apologizing: "I'm so not articulate today."

Soon after, we were called to photograph a Teen Vogue cover. It was the first time I detected a distinct sense of competition among the girls. Or perhaps it was just me? I was still dealing with that second-place mentality, especially after Dontay proposed to Jasmine. The entire photo shoot felt like an uneasy dance, with everyone wanting to support one other while also seizing the opportunity for press and visibility. The more attention the event received, the more it felt like we were all thrown into a game of flaming dodgeball, with everyone hoping to make it out alive. We were all so young and inexperienced, with no mature adult around to guide us through all of the nuanced and complex emotions that arose in our work dynamic.

I should have sought advise and reassurance from the hair and cosmetics Mama Bears, but years of being in these charismatic environments had instilled in me the belief that Christians had the ultimate answers and that we should not listen to nonbelievers. This was exacerbated by the slow boil I was experiencing, as I had been indoctrinated not to trust anyone outside of the Big House Family. On top of that, I felt embarrassed to be so self-centered. Everyone in the cast and crew deserved recognition and appreciation for their efforts. The show's success was due to more than just the five of us. It was due to all of us—every single person's distinct and significant contribution. How could I complain about the oddity of all this attention? Oh, are your glass slippers too tight? And I didn't want to share my insecurities with anyone in the Family because none of them, including Harker, had experienced this kind of renown. I knew they couldn't completely grasp. Worse, I was concerned that Les would interpret this as proof that I still wanted to be validated by Hollywood—which I did. I aspired to have a successful film and stage career, doing what I loved and knew I was meant to do. However, the new guilt cycle that Les had built around my desire for approval from anybody other than God—via the Big House Family—weighed hard on me. I couldn't tell the difference between a desire that God had placed within me and a "sinful desire" that was replacing God.

I wanted to call Mina to chat about how she was feeling now that she'd given up acting, but ever since I overheard Les tell Kurt over Christmas that she was bipolar, she and I had been drifting away. I didn't really understand what "bipolar" meant. This was in the early 2000s, when the word was much more stigmatized than it is today. I was still years away from receiving my own neurodivergent diagnosis. More than the term itself, Les's style of saying it implied that Mina was unstable and untrustworthy. I wasn't sure what to believe. I walked around in mental circles trying to figure out what was going on with my career, but the disorientation was not limited to that.

When the program traveled to Myrtle Beach to record an episode about a cheerleading competition, I met Ben, a gorgeous guy with curly blond hair who was staying at our hotel. He was a Christian who lived in Wilmington and was in town for a construction project. That's correct, I found a cute Christian carpenter. Aside from the similarities to Jesus, it just took a few dates for him to confess his love, and this level of decisiveness was intoxicating after all those years of Blue Eyes playing games. It was easy to forget about my disappointment at Jasmine's engagement in the presence of Ben. I barely knew him, but it didn't matter. We did not laugh at the same things, but it didn't matter. We did not like the same music, movie, or books, but that didn't matter. We both desired to be in love, therefore we chose to be in love. A month later, he proposed to me using candles, rose petals, and a ring I would never have selected. And I said yes despite my gut feeling that I should say no. I would will this to be correct.

Ben and I flew to Idaho for the weekend. He met everyone at the Big House, and Les and Pam eventually took him off for a discussion without me. Ben was classy and didn't mention what they said, and I didn't ask since I was scared the whole event was too heated and didn't want to make a big deal out of it and potentially give him second thoughts. But the day after we got back to Wilmington, the two of them called me.

"If this is the man you truly love and are confident in, then we love and support you," Pam stated. But... I'm not sure how compatible you two are."

"You're from two different worlds," Les replied. "You know, you have a lot of life experience, whereas he has only ever lived in that small village. And where will you live? He already has a great business locally. I do not see him moving up here."

"I just don't see it," Pam replied.

"Yeah, this doesn't feel right to me, either, baby," she replied. "But it's your decision."

After we hung up, I prayed for strength and went straight to visit Ben. He greeted me with delight, knowing how important their blessing was to me. In humiliation, I exploited that to avoid having to admit the truth: that I didn't love him after all, that my attraction had worn off now that I had his devotion, that I didn't know what was wrong with me, why I was so fickle, or why I only desired things I couldn't have. I didn't have to be honest because I had a way out.

"Everyone liked you, Ben. But I chatted with Les and Pam, and I think they're correct. I believe we rushed into this and should take a

step back.
"Do we take a step back or split up?" Ben inquired.
"I don't know," I replied.
I knew. I didn't want to harm him anymore than I already had. No. This is a lie I told myself. I didn't want to confront whatever was broken within me that allowed me to be so cold as to shift my emotions overnight. Literally overnight. I returned the ring to him, leaving him perplexed and extremely heartbroken.
After our trip to Idaho, the cast and crew noticed I was not wearing my ring the next week. The Mama Bears questioned me about it. As with my anxieties about sharing the attention with my co-stars, I didn't say much and kept my response brief. However, given the timing, it was easy to extrapolate that I ended my relationship with him because my "family" disapproved. They knew me well enough by this point to know I never did anything without the Family's permission.
It was around this time that the true murmurs began.

After Ben, I became increasingly skeptical about my ability to make sound judgments, so I began to seek guidance from Les and Pam on a regular basis—not only for my personal life but also for my profession. Les, in particular, was already doing this with everyone else, so the simple act of falling in line made me feel more connected to the group as a whole. When Abe performed with his band, Les always made sure to have a few family members along. He eventually persuaded Abe to change the band's roster, replacing the guitar and bass players with Miguel (who was actually very excellent) and one of the Barbarians (who was not). When Harker booked a movie, Les would accompany him on location as a "prayer intercessor" to provide spiritual support, and he even began creating a film script with him. It was about warriors, of course. He would offer to read audition sections with me while I was home for the weekend and was happy to provide input on any new songs or screenplays I was working on to pass the time. He also identified a female wedding vocalist with whom he suggested I form a band (which I temporarily did).
Les also established a business management company. It would handle the finances for Ed's medical business, assist Abe's band in keeping track of tour sales and expenses, and, of course, manage the

motel. He named it TRIAD, which stands for Trinity Redemption Investment and Asset Directors. Now that Les was mentoring artists, he embraced his own artistic side and created business cards in maroon and gold with that dreadful Papyrus font, as well as a very bad website. The website's "About" section described his title as "Leadership Development" and his specialty as "spiritual advising, conflict resolution, and vision casting." "Vision casting" was his term for whiteboarding or brainstorming. Pam had accounting skills from Ed's office, and Kurt had been running his plumbing business for three decades, thus they somehow gained the designation of accountant. Juana was also involved, albeit indirectly, as TRIAD used the bank where she worked. But, bizarrely, Gretchen was hired as bookkeeper and assistant. I had no idea how she would manage anyone's books when, as far as I knew, she had never worked, gotten a paycheck, or balanced a checkbook, and couldn't even keep her room clean. But Les wanted to boost Gretchen's confidence, and as a dyscalculic who had always had a business manager handle her finances, I didn't want to pass judgment.

I had a lot going on at work anyway. I was writing music in my spare time and regularly sung to myself on set, which led to numerous requests to sing on One Tree Hill. In one episode, Sheryl Crow made a special appearance, and Haley is so taken by her that she can't articulate a meaningful sentence. I felt the same paralysis-in-desire reaction when I met Sheryl that I did when I first met Moira Kelly. I was so frightened that all I could say was a brief hello, but what I really wanted to say was: Hi, I know every word in every song you've written, and I want to be just like you.

As a result of my performances on the show, I met with record labels and performed a showcase at the House of Blues in Los Angeles. Then, in early 2005, I was requested to be the opening act for a One Tree Hill concert tour of thirty-five cities with enormous venues. There would be tour busses and a supporting band; I'd get to perform my own songs in front of thousands of people across the United States. The tour featured Gavin DeGraw, Michelle Branch's Wreckers band, and Tyler Hilton, who had recently joined One Tree Hill as the humorous and villainous character Chris Keller after playing Elvis in the Oscar-winning film Walk the Line. On tour, Tyler and I competed like two children in a potato sack race. We were already singing and recording together in Wilmington for our characters' storylines, but we became close friends on the tour. Despite not sharing my faith or family, I developed a love on him while writing songs on the bus and in dressing rooms, watching Jim Henson's Labyrinth or The Princess Bride at midnight, and eating street tacos after a concert.

At the Portland stop, some of the Big House Family attended the show. Just like during my twenty-first birthday party, it was an opportunity for the Family to mingle with my non-Family friends. Warner Bros. flew a cast member to each tour stop to host the show. Paul Johansson was deployed to Portland. While Les focused on bonding with Tyler, whom he considered as a threat since he suspected I had a thing on him, Pam set her eyes on Paul.

Pam, Paul, and I headed to a diner near the performance venue after the show to have burgers. I think our chat went nicely. The tone remained pleasant—unlike Pam's chats with my mother and Camille's mother—and I hoped Paul would now see how beautiful and harmless the Family was and would be able to vouch for me on set when people muttered about the weirdness of the circumstances.

But when Pam departed, Paul told me, "Boy, she's very careful with her words, isn't she?""

"What do you mean?""I asked.

"It was intriguing talking to her. She is very deliberate about what she does and does not say. It seemed similar to filming a scene with a well-rehearsed actor. I mean, she is pretty. It is not a criticism, but rather an observation.

Paul was attempting to be pleasant, but it was evident that he did not regard Pam as a warm and genuine friend, as I did, which was disheartening. I had wanted to begin blending my two worlds.

As the tour progressed, Tyler seemed to want more separation from me. Instead of remaining up and talking to me on the bus, he went to bed early. When I invited him to go explore the local culinary scene like we typically do, he stated he had already made plans with the other tour participants. I had no idea why until he called me in my hotel room one night.

"Listen, this is awkward, but there's some rumors about you that my tour manager says someone might print in Us Weekly, and my name is attached because we've been hanging out so much, and—"

"Wait, slow down," I instructed. "What rumors?""

"Are you involved in a religious cult or something?"

I gave a long sigh. This world simply cannot comprehend the idea of a group of people committed to a genuine connection. It's very sad. "No, Ty. "I'm not in a cult."
"Okay, well... All your friends that I met seem nice, but..." I could tell this was difficult for him. "I do not know. "I just wanted to make sure you were okay."
Us Weekly never printed anything, and Tyler always treated me properly after that, but I despised having it hover over us. He'd become a terrific buddy, crush or no crush, and it stung to see others distance themselves from me.

New York was one of the tour's final stops. I was so delighted to return to my favorite city and feel at home again, but what made it even more thrilling was the news that my boss called me with before we arrived.
"They are interested in you because of Belle!" she stated.
"Wait," I asked. "On Broadway? How about Beauty and the Beast on Broadway?"
"Yes! I've been pitching you, but the tour's success has helped them understand the potential of One Tree Hill among their target audience. They want to see you reading. Can you go in before leaving New York?"
I was ecstatic at the idea of realizing my longstanding ambition. "Yes. Obviously. But we will leave tomorrow night."
"Okay, I will inform them. Simply work on the material. I emailed it to you. And be prepared to go in tomorrow morning. If everything goes well, they'll invite you back for a work session and then to see producers in a few weeks after your tour ends."
I did my fastest set that night so I could get back to the bus and begin practicing the material. As usual, the baker arrives with his tray. The following day, I completed my reading successfully. I was to return in three weeks, ready for the final producer session.
The first people I told were the Mama Bears in Wilmington. Everyone in the hair and makeup trailer came to a halt, yelped with delight, hugged me, and expressed their pride. Then I contacted my mother and father. They both broke down in tears because they were so thrilled for me.
At the time, I didn't think it was weird that I told the Mama Bears and my biological parents before telling Les. My hair and makeup

friends were just as into Broadway as I was. That's really all we talked about. I knew they'd understand what a major thing this was. And, while I wasn't saying much to my parents—especially since they had just started referring to the Family as a "cult"—they knew this had been a desire of mine since I started acting, and they had been the first ones to urge me to pursue that dream. I now see that I waited to inform Les because I was afraid about what he might say. And I was correct.

"What I feel in my spirit is that you're at a crossroads," Les said on the phone after I eventually told him. "One path leads to a job that will be extremely rewarding. One path leads to family, which will likewise be abundantly blessed. But I'll tell you what breaks my heart: you never got the opportunity to be a part of a family. You have been on the road for several months. This is the longest you've been away from us, and we're waiting with open arms. It's worth contemplating that this could be the enemy's strategy to keep you from your spiritual birthright as a child of God—pressing into Family and experiencing what it's like to truly be a member of heaven on Earth."

We were having this talk while I was on break from set. I was pacing in circles on an underused area of our property that was directly next to the airport and a military post, so there were often jets passing overhead.

"I mean, baby, you can't out-give God," Les told me.

"What do you mean?" I asked.

"Well, He is the giver of all good things." So, if you make this sacrifice for Him, He'll just turn it around and offer you something greater and better. It may not appear how you expect, but He will always turn a tithe into a blessing. We can tithe our dreams the same way we tithe our money.

I saw an outbound plane as the sun reflected off the metal. Perfectly white clouds against a blue sky. A little breeze. I wanted to go on that plane and be taken back to New York right away, with no time to think—because I felt myself giving in.

"That makes sense, I guess."

"If you go to New York, it will be huge for you. Everyone will notice how talented you are, and your career will take off in ways you cannot fathom. But I'm not sure where that leaves you spiritually. And I don't want you to receive a gift that you won't be able to properly manage, as I know being a member of this Family can provide. I know you'll make the correct choice, and it may be selfish of me, but I really want you to stay on the ship with us."

I surely did not want to pursue a dream at the cost of my spirit. But the idea of giving this up after a lifetime of desiring it scared me. I planned to give myself a few weeks to process, but I didn't even get that long. The following days, every time I phoned someone in Idaho, they refused to pick up, call, or text me back. I'd never had that happen in all of my years with the group. At first, I assumed people were merely busy, but it soon became clear that they were avoiding me, just as I had begun to avoid Mina after Les referred to her as bipolar. Maybe that's how everyone feels about me now, I thought. It was a good method to demonstrate what I would be missing if I prioritized my work over my family.

So now I was separated from both my One Tree Hill pals and my Idaho family. In my journal, I wrote, "It is so lonely." I hate being this lonely. Which dream is more important to me: Broadway or family?

It felt too shallow to consider. The response had to be "family." I had wanted a family for longer than I had wanted Broadway. Family was the bigger dream. If I could let go of Blue Eyes, I could also let go of this.

I called my manager. She was stunned and attempted to talk me out of it. She said she'd check back in a few days to see if I had changed my mind. I did not. She reluctantly contacted casting, explaining that there was a scheduling conflict and that I would be unable to do the job. When I told the Mama Bears and my parents, they were equally startled. They attempted to talk me out of it, but just like my broken engagement to Ben, I pretended everything was alright. "It's just not in alignment with me right now," I told myself. But when I was alone in my flat, I became ill with loss. I grieved and yelled more than I did when I finished with Blue Eyes because, forget TV, Broadway was THE dream I'd had since I was a child. And it wasn't just my dream; Grandma Doris had one as well. Walking away from that opportunity was a permanent betrayal of her and my entire ancestry, as well as myself.

When I began to recover from my depression over this, my next call was to Mina. I wasn't sure if what Les had said about her was accurate, but I knew she was my friend. I missed her, and if I'd made her feel the way I did when the Family ignored me, I needed to make up. She was grateful and said she had been perplexed as to why we hadn't been as close recently. I didn't want to betray Les, so I told her I was preoccupied with work. But when I told her about Beauty and the Beast, she was horrified for me.

Joy, why didn't you accept it? We would all have backed you! Take it!"Of course it was too late. In the years after I left the Family, I've wondered if Les's purpose for discouraging me from taking on the job was financial. Perhaps he believed that pursuing a job on Broadway would imperil my position on—and compensation from—One Tree Hill. Perhaps he saw Broadway as a detour from more lucrative TV or film gigs. Probably it was part of it. But I think it was more easier than that. If I relocated to New York and realized my Broadway ambition, there was a high possibility I would never return. He would have been correct, too! The woman who took Belle's place was discovered and went on to play another of my dream roles, Mary Poppins, in Cameron Mackintosh's production. I'd have been back on the path Grandma Doris had envisioned, and Les would have had one fewer person to manipulate. He couldn't let it happen. Because, despite his murky financial activities (which would eventually become even shadier), Les was far more concerned with control than money.

CHAPTER NINETEEN

Emily told me about a group of swingers who wanted to rent the motel and conference center for a weekend. Although the money was much needed, she declined, believing it was misaligned with the motel's ministry purpose. Kurt disagreed, arguing that it was an opportunity to reach lost souls. Against Emily's objections, he called the swingers back to finalize the booking. The decision led to Emily's demotion, with Les justifying it as correcting the "mistake" of putting a woman in a leadership position.

The group's handling of sexual behavior showed double standards. Dontay, a maintenance worker, was caught watching porn and faced public shaming, eviction, and a broken engagement with Jasmine, despite being one of the Family's most devoted members. Yet, paying strangers engaging in debauchery were welcomed because of the financial benefit.

Financial struggles hit the group hard. Mina, pregnant again, sold her BMW under pressure and replaced it with an unreliable Dodge. When the car failed, Ed stepped in to help, causing tension with Les, who believed hardships were lessons. Ed quietly apologized for "meddling," reflecting the pervasive control Les exerted.

Les and Pam ran a counseling practice despite lacking formal credentials. Their methods often created divisions. Les, portraying himself as a wise leader, advised Mina against trusting Harker and subtly sought to influence relationships. Harker, increasingly frustrated, began challenging Les's authority, questioning teachings like the term "covenant family." This resistance exposed cracks in the group's unity.

Pirelli, a so-called prophet, held a sold-out workshop at the motel, drawing attendees nationwide. Les used Pirelli's presence to boost his credibility, further isolating the Family from external criticism. Any dissent was dismissed as spiritual attacks, reinforcing the group's insular mindset. Joy's engagement to QB stemmed from mounting pressure rather than love. Caught kissing, QB was pushed to propose. Joy, conflicted and desperate to preserve her place in the Family, agreed despite her doubts. Les and Pam framed obedience over emotions as God's will, convincing her to proceed. Joy abandoned her instincts, sold her LA apartment, and tied her finances to QB. Despite her efforts, her wedding day brought no joy, only numbness, underscoring her internal struggle to reconcile faith, fear, and identity.

CHAPTER TWENTY

I married QB in a freezing barn on an apple orchard, wearing a Justina McCaffrey dress I'd purchased alone from Kleinfeld in New York. My mom wasn't there when I bought it and wasn't with me when I put it on in a cold side room, trying not to trip over old space heaters. Pam had fully inserted herself as my "spiritual mother," and since the Big House Family took precedence over my biological family, my mom was treated like a guest. Pam didn't even speak to her. She'd essentially replaced her. Whoever was in charge of propane didn't buy enough, so my poor grandmother was shivering along with the rest of the fifty-plus guests. Thankfully, Juana had the sense to buy blankets the day before, which people could grab on their way in. Walking down the aisle felt like acting in a play. Standing at the altar as Les married us felt like being in a scene I'd done before. I'd stood at an altar multiple times on TV: marrying Paul Anthony Stewart's character on *Guiding Light* and James Lafferty's Nathan Scott on *One Tree Hill*. I knew how to play this part.I looked at QB, then out at the audience, wondering if I was allowed to break the fourth wall in this show. In my mind, I pictured Blue Eyes standing at the back, striding down the aisle to stop the wedding and whisk me away. But this wasn't make-believe—this was my life. Les skipped the "if anyone has good cause" part, probably knowing some people in the room might actually stand up for me. After saying our "I dos," we walked back down the aisle to Dusty Springfield's *"Son of a Preacher Man"* and had a reception featuring middling lasagna, carrot cake, and a chocolate fountain. I drank enough champagne to forget most of it.For our honeymoon, QB drove me to the airport but didn't reveal the destination until we were inside. I'd dropped so many hints about wanting to go somewhere exciting like Paris or Iceland, but when I saw the ticket, I couldn't believe it: Colorado. It was Les's idea—a deal at a struggling lodge that had been in the news for Kobe Bryant's trial the year before. Worse, QB hadn't even paid for it; he used my money, just as he'd done since we'd merged our accounts. The least he could've done was put me on a beach. But Les raised his sons to believe marriage was all about sex, and QB parroted this idea: "We're not really gonna leave the room anyway."As a good Christian girl saving myself for marriage, I had always been told sex would be amazing once I found "the one." Instead, intimacy with someone I had no desire for felt confusing and deeply sad. I had hoped it would bring us closer, but it only pushed us further apart. I was angry at him for treating me like an object, and he was angry that the evangelical purity-culture promises about wives being a "reward" were false. By the end of the first week, I felt trapped. He didn't want to go sightseeing or try snowmobiling. Even when I offered to ski, he insisted we stay in the room.I needed to break the monotony, so I convinced him to take a walk. We found a frozen lake and an old hut with decorative vintage ice skates. They fit my feet, so I skated topless to make him laugh. "Come on," I said, "let's skinny-skate!" He laughed at first, then panicked someone might see us. His embarrassment sucked all the fun out of the moment. His playfulness, which had been one of the few things I enjoyed about him, had vanished. We walked back to the hotel in silence and barely left the room for the rest of the trip. After the honeymoon, QB moved to Wilmington with me, where he began "integrating" our lives. He monitored where I went, what I wore, and who I talked to. He even made me purge clothes and keepsakes from my life before marriage. We moved into a beige apartment overlooking a shopping center—soulless, like our relationship. On set, my castmates were cordial to him, but he mistrusted them and called them frauds behind their backs. His controlling behavior escalated: he wanted to review my scripts, approve my wardrobe, and dictate my interactions with male colleagues. I was too young to recognize this as abusive and justified his actions as "spiritual leadership." I confided in Harker and Mina, admitting I felt trapped and that our marriage had been a mistake. They were supportive, but when I shared this with QB, he exploded, forbidding me from talking to anyone else about our issues. Les's doctrine of "unity" was used to justify his control over me. I became numb to survive. In a bid to reclaim some joy, I threw myself into a passion project: adapting *The Notebook* into a musical. Partnering with Ron Aniello, I poured my heart into the production. The workshop was a success, but TRIAD's interference and cult rumors caused Broadway producers to pull out. The rights were sold to someone else, leaving me devastated. Les shifted focus to buying a local restaurant, the Bistro, using my money and that of other Family members. The motel, a financial failure, was abandoned, but Les framed it as a spiritual success. I invested in the Bistro, hoping it might salvage my marriage, but TRIAD's mismanagement and constant demands for funds drained me further. Over the next three years, I spiraled deeper into emotional numbness. Even sex became a scheduled "duty" Les counseled us to perform, further eroding my sense of self. I convinced myself I needed to obey, but inside, I was dying. By 2010, I thought having a baby might fix things, but the cracks in my marriage and life were too wide to ignore. Slowly, I began to see the light breaking through.

PART THREE

CHAPTER TWENTY ONE

Another basement meeting was scheduled, this time for Gretchen. She sat on the middle seat, surrounded by the family.

"As you guys know," Gretchen continued, "I've been in charge of TRIAD's bookkeeping. "And, um..." She started crying. Pam went to sit at Gretchen's feet and stroked her legs. Gretchen spoke slowly. "I'm very sorry. I've been spending the money to gamble. I kept thinking I could make it bigger, but it just grew worse." Her sorrow evolved into wailing.

Pam continued to touch her, adding, "I'm so proud of you."

The room was silent. Gretchen said, "QB and Joy, I took the most from you."

By this point, I'd been sufficiently trained that the only appropriate answer was to forgive her. Immediately. I was certain that I was so selfish that I had no right to look down on others. I had no right to be angry. I paid no attention to my own sentiments or emotions. On the contrary, I wanted to demonstrate the compassion I believed was demanded of a Christian. Pam was modeling the behavior we were supposed to exhibit for Gretchen at this time. I watched her cry and understood how it felt to be ashamed. But as I began to talk, QB spoke first.

"It's okay, Gretch," he said. "Everyone makes errors. "I forgive you."

I became outraged.

It was not Q's money. That was my. There was nothing he could forgive. And why didn't he get outraged on my behalf? I had seen him become enraged over little perceived infractions on numerous occasions. I disrespected him by asking so many questions. I neglected to express my plans, thus he felt ignored. I'd refuse to give in to a fight because I so much wanted him to simply understand me rather than demand my cooperation. He was gradually adopting his father's habit of throwing or smashing things when I didn't listen or comprehend him the way he wanted. However, it was when it was just the two of us. When it was only us, he was a tough guy. Now that he was surrounded by the rest of the Family and confronted with a true crime that justified his rage and aggression, all he could offer was meekness. I was more outraged by his lame statement than by the theft itself. Even in my rage, I was scared to make the situation about "our" concerns.

I jumped up almost robotically and rushed up to Gretchen, hugging her. "Love you, sis," I said.

Her confession appeared to be over before it started. Nobody inquired how much she stole. I still do not know. It had to be enormous; else, I'm sure TRIAD would have hidden it. There was no talk of reimbursement. There was no outcry at the betrayal of a dear friend and confidante, who used our money to fuel her addiction. It was just "Let's move on."

Perhaps as a result of this theft—and the knowledge that the more individuals let into the Family, the more difficult it would be to supervise them all and the simpler it would be for such deception—Les quickly stated that no more people would be admitted.

"I've been praying about this," he said, "and I believe the Lord is telling me that this covenant Family is complete and whole today. "No one new will come in unless they are married or born here."

The timing of this specific order was strange, and it made me question if Les was even more of a prophet than his Welsh friend Pirelli. Just a few days later, I discovered I was pregnant.

The metal laundry basket incident occurred while I was six months pregnant. Who knows why we were fighting at the time. It was probably the state of our house when I arrived home from one of the last flights I'd be able to take at that point in my pregnancy. The magnificent new house I had purchased was beginning to resemble the Big House. The floors were filthy, the bathroom sink was covered in weeks of toothpaste spit, clothes piles filled the bedroom, and the kitchen had a mound of dishes and pots so unclean that the crusted food was moldy, leftover from a dinner he'd served weeks before.

Whatever triggered the fight, QB had a fit and slammed the metal laundry basket against the wall, leaving dents in the drywall and feces on the floor from our terrified Yorkshire terrier, who scampered into the bedroom to hide after discharging himself. I asked Emily to come over since I was so disturbed up. She arrived to see broken pots and planters all over the front porch, which Q had crushed before driving away.

Emily walked in and discovered me picking up broken glass from picture frames.

"Oh my god, Joy," she exclaimed. "Are you okay?"

I actually wasn't. I'd been through this for five years of marriage. I was pregnant and afraid, and I couldn't hide it any longer.

Emily picked up a tiny end table that had been knocked over in the chaos of the room. "I had no idea he got angry like this," she told me. No one does, I reasoned. He is a quiet boy. He's the world's kindest person.

I burst into tears. I slumped onto the couch, still holding the broom and dustpan, my tummy pressing against my thighs.

She sat next me. "Does this happen a lot?" she inquired.

"It's not usually like this," I said, hoping to shield him. "This is the biggest mess he's ever made."

"I don't think it matters if it's generally this way or not. This is a significant issue. "This is not okay, Joy."

She wrapped her arm around me.

"I'm very sorry," she said. "I had no idea."

"You've got your own stuff to deal with," I told you. Abe had been experiencing unusual bouts of vertigo and was diagnosed with "pars planitis," a condition in which his retina would randomly detach, resulting in vision loss and vertigo. "How is he doing?"

"He just needs to be careful," Emily remarked. "The biggest threat isn't vision loss; it's him falling down and striking his skull when his eyes go black. The doctor indicated the most important thing he has to avoid is sharp hits to the head. This could significantly worsen the problem, even resulting in permanent blindness. So I'll have to quit beating up on him."

She frowned as soon as she uttered it, briefly forgetting why she was there. I smiled at her, making it plain that I took no offense.

At that time, I felt a searing pain in my stomach, like if all of my muscles were clenching around the baby. I winced, groaned, and struggled to breathe.

"What is it?" Emily inquired.

"I'm not sure. Oh, God, this is extremely painful."

"Can you walk to the car?"

"Yes, I guess so. Yeah." The anxiety and pain were all mixed up now. We got to Emily's car, and she took me to the hospital. Coldplay's "Fix You" played on the radio like a terrible movie cliché, and I glanced out the window, attempting to be strong but failing.

The baby was all right. The pain was caused by early Braxton-Hicks contractions, most likely triggered by stress. A few hours later,

Emily drove me home, and Q's car was back in the driveway. When I entered the house, the first thing I noticed was a clump of dog poo that he hadn't bothered to clean up.

Rosie was born in Wilmington. I wanted Pam to be present for the birth because she had attended all of the Family births. Mina, Jasmine, Emily—none of their biological mothers were permitted in the room, but Pam assisted with every delivery. Except mine. She was preoccupied with her own grandchildren, so Les and Marti came out to help. Les entered the birthing room to pray over me, and the nurses praised him as a great man. "Your baby is so lucky to have a grandfather like that."

Martine's presence was beneficial and relaxing. I requested Shantel VanSanten to videotape the birth so I could have photographic recollections. Shantel played my sister, Quinn, on One Tree Hill. She had been friendly and open since she joined the cast in Season 7. I'd never felt judged by her, and we'd come so close. QB was also fantastic. He knew all the pressure points and sat beside my bed, massaging me. In my lucid moments of noticing him bring me water or hold my hand, I had flashbacks of our happy days together. I stayed up late drinking wine and laughed at a TV show. A quick trip to the Bahamas, where we swam with dolphins and actually saw Julia Roberts in the hotel, allowing me to confirm her name for him in real time. Playing board games. An occasional flower bouquet. He wrote me letters on parchment paper using a genuine quill and ink. He was a romantic at heart—if only I didn't get in his way. It wasn't all horrible, I reminded myself, hoping for more of those good days now that we had a baby to care for.

It's a terrible feeling to be handed this fragile tiny human, all squishy and gooey with a million working parts, any of which may stop operating in a split second, and it's up to you to keep the gears turning. I began to trust God in a new manner. It's not the same as giving up my dreams and expecting He'll bring something else back. This is not the same as trusting Him to answer my prayers for a successful marriage.

This level of trust was equivalent to waking up every day in an abandoned well—the kind that kids used to fall down in the 1980s— and hoping that someone would find you. I felt completely helpless, relying on a God in whom I had lost so much faith to provide me with daily knowledge, patience, calm, and rest. But I had no option, and at the end of each day, no matter how messed up, I always felt like I'd been given the rope I needed.

Mom paid a visit after the birth. She stayed in Wilmington for several weeks, patiently assisting as I vented my frustrations with QB on her. My hormones did not help. I was an emotional explosion, but Mom suppressed her want to yell back at me like she did when I was younger. She was respectful rather than demanding, and inquiring rather than critical. It was a surprising display of self-control, and it contributed significantly to my growing faith and reliance on her. During that time, I turned thirty. No champagne fountains. Just an evening at home with Mom, Rosie, and QB. He gave me a store-bought card this time, rather than a handcrafted one.

We were barely three months away from concluding One Tree Hill permanently. When I went to work to finish the last few episodes, the Mama Bears surprised me with an impromptu baby shower. I was given the lovely rocking rocker that my character Haley nursed her baby daughter in during the previous season. Sophia and Austin Nichols (who played her love interest, filmmaker Julian Baker), gifted us an amazingly soft blanket with Rosie's name and birthday embroidered on it. Daphne Zuniga, another '90s TV icon who had joined the show to play Brooke Davis' amazing mother, sent me a bottle of champagne that was entirely suitable for the character. "For later," she added with a wink. And there was so much more—an outpouring of love for me and my new girlfriend. I recall being startled by the support I received because I had created an emotional wall against everyone. It was a humbling experience.

Q moved back to Wilmington full-time, intending to care for Rosie while I was at work. She had to stay near since I was feeding her, and she had a tongue-tie, which made things more difficult. To keep her routine, Q needed to spend the majority of the day with her in my trailer. I would take pauses to nurse or pump, then return to work. Q spent his time playing video games and going walks with the infant. After a few weeks, he admitted that he "wasn't a babysitter" and that he was paying a nanny to go "do stuff" during the day. When I asked him what "stuff" was, understanding he meant going to the gym, he responded "restaurant stuff." It was difficult not to laugh.

According to interactions I had with Danielle, Dontay, and other family members, the restaurant was proving to be a disaster. Les had no idea how much money it takes to run a restaurant, and he and Kurt were constantly grumbling about the cost of everything. Miguel could cook well, but he lacked the necessary qualifications to run a professional kitchen. There weren't many other possibilities. Few experienced cooks wanted to relocate to the middle of nowhere Idaho. Les eventually found someone, but the chef lacked the funds to relocate or the credit to qualify for a mortgage. Les offered to buy him and his family a neighboring home to reside in! This I learned from Les himself, because "we buy" obviously meant "Joy buys." By now, I wasn't surprised that he told me rather than asking. No, what astonished me was that he actually told me. I suppose for the same reason as Gretchen's confession to theft: a sum that huge was bound to be recognized eventually.

On a follow-up contact with Jas and Dontay, they revealed that the chef was a disaster. He was very hostile to the personnel, was extremely sluggish to get dishes out of the kitchen, and had a drug issue. When several employees objected, Les replied, "This restaurant is a place of ministry, and rather than judging this man, we should be helping him get his life together."

"We're working our butts off, but it feels like quicksand," Jasmine commented.

"And everyone is freaking out about money," Dontay remarked. "Danielle was invited to cater a supper for twenty-five persons for Pop's Rotary Club meeting, and Pop paid her $100 to do so. He even yelled at me last week because I deposited the cash from the night rather than leaving it for Kurt to do."

"Please pray for us out here, Joy! "I think we're all tired of Pop being in charge of literally everything," Jasmine stated. "He's gotta be exhausted, too!"

When I thought of the dreadful carnival that awaited me back in Idaho, I was even sadder. One Tree Hill was almost over. The act had served as a barrier between me and QB, and I was frightened of facing a life with only him, finally together. I had been in Wilmington for nearly a decade, almost my entire twenties, under contract with Warner Bros. and portraying Haley James Scott. I'd even established my worth as a filmmaker and been asked back to direct many episodes, discovering creative satisfaction in a completely new area. Now that everything was coming to an end, I understood how uncommon and special the entire experience had been, and how I had failed to appreciate it in the years prior. For the last two weeks, I vowed to put my own issues aside and enjoy the remaining moments.

During the final week of filming, fans stormed the set, gathering around the sets with cameras. Cast members also came to the stages, even if they weren't filming, to watch and cheer on whoever was finishing their final scene. Mine took place on a rooftop that overlooks downtown Wilmington. My on-screen kid, Jackson Brundage, ripped a loose stone out of a wall where Haley and Lucas used to store future forecasts and keep them hidden from the outside world. Haley was now pondering on the passage of time and making new forecasts with her young son.

"This is a magical spot, son. I've noticed the beauty in your eyes for the past nine years. "There is only one Tree Hill, Jamie Scott, and it is your home."

These were my final words as Haley James Scott. Before they said cut, I performed a lyric from the musical Sunset Boulevard, not for the episode, but for everyone who had made their own sacrifices to be a part of this show throughout the years, including the writers and editors who would be watching from Los Angeles.

I don't know why I'm frightened,
I know my way around here,
The cardboard trees, the painted scenes, the sound here.
. . . .
We'll have early morning madness.
We'll have magic in the making.
Yes, everything's as if we never said goodbye...

And that was all. Our executive producer and regular director, Greg Prange, said, "Cut! Ladies and gentlemen, the series concludes with our amazing, gorgeous Bethany Joy Lenz." He may have said more, as it was customary for him to say a few brief words, but I cannot recall them. I only remember holding back tears. I wish I had allowed myself to cry the way I wanted to, but I had grown so accustomed to numbness that when I felt tears welling up, I tamped them down, scared that if I let them out, I would never be able to stop.

I got into Paul's car about an hour later, after finishing up with my trailer. Though QB's disapproval meant we couldn't be as close in recent years as we had been early in the show, we both agreed it would be good to have one final supper. QB granted me permission, despite the fact that I merely asked for it performatively. I was leaving whether he liked it or not.

"Jesus, what a day!" Paul said. "Oh, I apologize for using that word. 'Day.' " He smirked. A dad's long-standing joke about curse words.

"How do you feel?" I asked him.

"Oh, Joy. "You understand." He paused and inhaled sharply, his reliable warning that an elegantly stated thought was about to emerge. "...We're all fucking tired."

I laughed.

"How are you feeling?" You are the one with the new baby! "You're about to return home and begin a new chapter in your life!"

I watched gorgeous, charming Wilmington pass by. Historic dwellings, Spanish moss, and graveyards On rare occasions, I would go through and envy the people who lived there. "It feels right for the journey to be ending," I told myself. "Yes, we're all tired..."

"But? "You sound like there's more."

Of course there is more! I want you and everyone I've said goodbye to in the last several weeks to grab hold of me and say, "We're your family. "Don't return to that awful place."

"No. "It will be nice to get home." Saying "home" did not feel the same as talking about Florida, Texas, New Jersey, New York, or Los Angeles. Home was now a rogue ship with terrified passengers. I altered the subject. "Sophia gave me The Alchemist."

"Excellent book. Did you get her anything?

"Yeah, I found this small wooden suitcase, so I decorated the whole inside like a—whaddya call those school projects inside a shoebox?"

"Diorama?"

"Yes! "Like a diorama with..." I paused. There was something I wanted to keep hidden about this one. Even though we never achieved the sisterly, yell-it-out-and-it's-still-okay connection we desired with one other, my heart expanded into a gigantic bear embrace for her. I adored Sophia and thought we'd get there one day. I told her not to open the suitcase and keep it on a shelf until she needed it. She would be aware of the situation as soon as it occurred.

"Saying goodbye on projects like these is so hard," Paul told me. "This is the longest I've been on a series, but I came in old already." He laughed. "You all grew up with this show! You pretended to have a husband for ten years! "How do you say goodbye to that?"

"I do not know. "James was the hardest to say goodbye to."
"Oh, I thought it would have been me." He smiled.
"Ha, well, ask me in an hour when dinner's over." I rolled down the window, and the cool air of winter blew in. "I was married to James for longer than I have been with QB. Well, Haley married Nathan.
"You understand what I mean."
"You get him anything?"
"I wrote him a card."
Even though James and I had a platonic real-world connection, my time on set with him appearing to be in a happy marriage provided me with a reprieve—perhaps even an example of what a happy existence could look like. I merely hugged him and handed him a card, bottled up my sentiments as I always did, wishing I knew how to communicate 10 years of thanks.
"Jesus, you coulda at least bought him a bottle of tequila," he added.
"Sorry, there's that word again." 'Tequila' "
When Paul dropped me off at my apartment after dinner, we both agreed to stay in touch. But I had a feeling that would be the last time we spoke. Fortunately—for both myself and my daughter—I was mistaken.

CHAPTER TWENTY TWO

The scene unfolding in my living room was one of chaos. Jasmine was pacing, her anger a palpable force that filled the room as she unleashed a torrent of revelations. The moment she told me about Dontay's confession—that he'd cheated on her weeks before their wedding and that Les had ordered him to keep it a secret—I was stunned. My brain struggled to process it all. The audacity, the manipulation—it was infuriating. Jasmine's rage was contagious, and soon I found myself consumed by anger as well. This wasn't just about Dontay or even Jasmine's heartbreak; it was about the system that allowed this betrayal to happen. Les had been pulling strings, orchestrating people's lives under the guise of divine intervention. It felt like every decision he made was a calculated move to maintain control, no matter the cost to those involved.

When Jasmine mentioned how Les had once told her she was at a "crossroads" and needed to stay with the Family, it hit me like a thunderbolt. He'd used the same words on me years earlier when I had turned down Broadway. The parallels were unnerving. Jasmine and I were pawns in his game, each manipulated into sacrificing our dreams for his agenda. Later that night, I confronted QB about it. His dismissive response was as predictable as it was infuriating. He brushed off Jasmine's anger as a misunderstanding and even went so far as to suggest she might be bipolar. It was gaslighting at its finest, and I could feel my trust in him—and in the Family—eroding further.

But the final blow came not from QB but from Harker and Mina. Their email arrived like a crack of lightning, illuminating the truth that had been lurking in the shadows. They had left the Family, breaking free from the suffocating grip of Les's control. Harker's words, "I do not want 'unity' at the expense of truth," resonated deeply with me. It was a lifeline, a glimmer of hope that escape was possible.

The fallout was immediate and ugly. The Family's response to Harker and Mina was a masterclass in spiritual manipulation, shaming them for daring to think independently. I had even signed the response letter, clinging desperately to the illusion of stability within the Family. But deep down, Harker's defiance planted a seed of doubt in me. Maybe, just maybe, there was a way out.

The softball field brawl was the breaking point. Watching Kurt punch Abe and seeing Emily leap to her husband's defense, only for Les to hold Abe down and whisper eerily in his ear—it was surreal. It was violence disguised as a Family dispute, and I couldn't unsee the truth: this wasn't a community. It was a cult.

The fallout from the brawl rippled through the Family, exposing fractures that had long been hidden. Abe, ever the patient peacemaker, began speaking out, questioning where our tithes were going and calling out the blatant hypocrisy. Les's red-faced tirade in response was both revealing and damning. The veneer of righteousness was cracking, and what lay beneath was far from holy.

When Martine showed up at my house, trying to force her way in under the guise of being "concerned," I realized just how far they were willing to go to keep me under their control. Her attempt to physically push past me was the last straw. As I slammed the door in her face, I knew there was no turning back.

The day I walked into the bank to withdraw my money was a pivotal moment. Juana, one of the few people from the Family I still trusted, showed me the account balance: $220,000. Two million dollars were missing, siphoned away under TRIAD's management. My body shook as I realized the extent of the betrayal. Juana helped me open a new account, her quiet professionalism masking the gravity of what she was risking to help me. That act of kindness gave me the strength to take the next step.

When Pam served me divorce papers, her fake sympathy only solidified my resolve. I wasn't just leaving QB; I was leaving the entire toxic system that had consumed my life. Packing up and moving to LA with Rosie was a logistical nightmare, but Danielle's unwavering support made it possible. Her defiance of Les's authority inspired me to keep pushing forward.

The custody battle that followed was brutal. The Family's intimidation tactics, from their parking lot standoffs to Martine's porch theatrics, were designed to break me. But I was done being a victim. I fought back with everything I had, determined to protect Rosie and reclaim my life.

In the end, the Family's greatest weapon—control—became their greatest weakness. They underestimated the power of truth and the resilience of someone who had finally seen through their facade. My journey out of the cult was far from over, but for the first time in years, I felt free. Free to rebuild, free to dream, and free to be the mother Rosie deserved.

CHAPTER TWENTY THREE

The conversation with my dad, that first time we reconnected, was unexpected in its simplicity. It wasn't about the cult or the pain I'd endured; it was just about love. He wanted me to know how much he loved and missed me, repeating it like a mantra that slowly stitched together the wounds I didn't even know were still bleeding. For all his faults—and God knew there were many—his love for me was something I couldn't doubt.

Yet, that love came with a sharp edge. When he visited me months later in West Hollywood, where I was trying to rebuild my life, he brought with him a bombshell in the form of a red folder. It was thick, heavy, and bursting with papers—documents he'd spent six years compiling. Inside was everything he'd uncovered about Les: lies, manipulation, financial exploitation, broken families, and even accusations of sexual misconduct.

I was stunned by how much effort my dad had poured into uncovering the truth. He hadn't just been angry or disappointed; he'd been driven. He'd dedicated years to understanding the cult's tactics and piecing together Les's history of destruction. It wasn't just about saving me; it was about holding Les accountable.

"This is how we get this motherfucker," he said with a determination that both terrified and inspired me.

The folder became my lifeline, not just in my custody battle but in my own journey toward healing. With each page, I realized how blind I'd been, how thoroughly Les had deceived us all. I was furious with myself for falling for it, but as I reached out to others who had been hurt by him, I began to see a different perspective. I wasn't alone in my gullibility. I wasn't uniquely stupid. I was human, like them, like all of us.

Through cold calls, emails, and letters, I built a network of survivors. Each conversation unearthed more of Les's atrocities and solidified my resolve. Some people were too scared to talk, their fear of Les still palpable even years later. Others, though hesitant at first, eventually opened up, sharing stories that mirrored my own pain and anger. And then there were those like Alice Burke, whose story brought a whole new level of horror to light.

Alice's testimony about Kurt—how she was groomed, drugged, and assaulted, and then sent back to her abuser by Les—was the final straw. It confirmed what I already suspected: there was no limit to Les's depravity. He didn't just enable monsters; he actively shielded them, ensuring their harm could continue unabated. Alice's courage in coming forward became a cornerstone of my case.

The custody battle was grueling, stretching on for three years and draining every ounce of my emotional and financial reserves. But with the evidence my dad had uncovered, the testimonies of Alice and others, and the support of friends who had seen my struggle, I finally won. The judge ruled in my favor, granting me custody of Rosie and ensuring she would never have to set foot in that toxic environment again.

But winning didn't feel like victory. It felt like survival. By the time the dust settled, I was a shadow of myself, exhausted and angry—not just at Les or Q or the Family, but at God. For years, I had followed every rule, made every sacrifice, trusted every so-called authority, and where had it gotten me? Nowhere. Worse than nowhere. It had taken everything from me.

One night, standing on my balcony in LA, the anger erupted. I screamed at God, cursed Him, demanded answers. My voice broke against the night air, my fury carrying with it a decade of pain and disillusionment. When I finally collapsed into a chair, spent and hopeless, the silence was deafening.

And then, out of nowhere, that memory returned—the sound of rain, the smell of bacon and coffee, the warmth of a diner booth on a rainy day when I was nineteen.

"Never doubt that I am real."

It wasn't a voice I heard; it was a presence I felt, one I had been chasing for years in all the wrong places. It was the same loving presence I'd felt back then, a quiet reassurance that, despite everything, I wasn't alone.

The realization hit me like a wave: that moment, all those years ago, had been real. It wasn't a trick of my imagination or a fleeting emotional high. It was real, and it had stayed with me, waiting for the moment I would need it most.

For the first time in years, I felt a glimmer of hope. Not because everything was suddenly okay—far from it. But because I knew, deep down, that I wasn't completely lost. There was a way forward, even if I couldn't see it yet. And maybe, just maybe, I wasn't walking it alone.

CHAPTER TWENTY FOUR

Part of the judge's decision was to separate custody from financial difficulties. To disentangle all of this, a new trial would be necessary. When we subpoenaed TRIAD's financial records, they were delivered in fifteen bankers boxes, jammed full and out of order.

"I've been doing this a long time," my forensic accountant told me over the phone following the ruling. "I understand what I am looking at. There's no doubt these folks are fraudsters who have completely plundered you blind."

I had moved to a less expensive rental in Studio City. It was on the corner where my bedroom window backed up to the Oyster Bar parking lot, and the lid of their dumpster bin was frequently left open, dangling over the rose shrub in our front "yard" (LA plot of grass). Rosie was four years old when she helped me fold clothes, which was one of her favorite "grown-up" pastimes. I stepped back so she couldn't hear the chat.

The forensic accountant spent ten minutes explaining how it worked—or tried to, at least. My thoughts went blank as she described what sounded like a spaghetti bowl of movements. She introduced me to a world I was unfamiliar with—since I was twelve, I had only had business managers (or my mother) handle any money-related matters. I didn't even realize I had a retirement account! "Falsified checks" and "501(c)(3)" and "cash infusion" and "guise of tithing" and "shell corporations" drifted through my disoriented haze, but I couldn't be sure I comprehended it all. The maneuvers were so complicated that looking through the paper trail archives still confuses me. My bewilderment was exacerbated by my self-loathing for being so naive and cowardly—for being so terrified to live my own life that I entirely surrendered my autonomy and let someone else take control of it. Yes, while the means weren't entirely evident to me at the time, the financial end result was that more than $2 million had been taken from my savings account. Despite this realization, I continued to think the way Les had taught me: excusing him and blaming myself.

"I've already sent a letter to the Idaho state district attorney's office, requesting that they take on the case as a matter of public safety," my accountant remarked, bringing me back into the present. "But, even though we have the overall numbers and basic trails to piece together the story, we still need to show the concrete evidence, receipt by receipt, bank statement by bank statement." Based on the number of bank accounts, the amount of money flowing around, and all of the other people involved, I estimate that it will take me and my team between 200 and 500 hours to comb through everything and provide an airtight case. I would LOVE to take on this project, but even at a lowered cost, you'll still be paying at least $100,000, if not more. And it doesn't include legal fees for seeking subpoenas, taking more depositions, or actually appearing in court."

I wasn't even sure how I'd pay the rent in a few months. I was receiving two or three minor jobs a year: short arcs on Dexter, Colony, and Grey's Anatomy; a Lifetime Christmas movie; and a low-budget action film that didn't get distributed. The forensic accountant read my stillness and proceeded.

"Look, I'm going to take this case and get these folks. What they did to you was unconscionable, and I would gladly see them all imprisoned. But may I give you personal advice?

"Of course," I replied.

"Walk away," she urged. "You have your daughter. You've been fighting these demons for three years—almost her entire life. You're aware of the toll this has had on your health. I am sure it has had an impact on your connection with your daughter, even if only subconsciously. Going after them like this will not be easy. You're looking at at least another year, possibly longer. And they are litigious and contentious. They'll probably try to make your life worse than it already is. Don't let them take away any more of your peace. Take your lovely girl and start your life over."

I looked back at Rosie, who was folding laundry. Her deep little voice reached out to me, "Mama!" "I found a button." She was laughing and waving it in the air.

"So, just let him get away with it?" asked I. "Give him even more money in mediation—money that should be for Rosie?"

Q's solicitors presented a mediation deal in which he would receive half of my retirement account, which my mother and professional business managers had reportedly been contributing to since I was twelve and began acting professionally. He'd also receive approximately $10,000 per year until Rosie was eighteen in order to "repay" half of the money I withdrew when I separated our accounts. And he'd get one of the cars, and I'd take on the debt from the short sale of the house.

"There's always a chance the DA's office will take the case," the forensic accountant stated. "Some of the money has been sent across state borders, which may make this a federal case. You can let things go at your end and leave it to the authorities."

My stomach churned, and my throat felt heated. Rage rushed through me. Then, across the room, Rosie stumbled from the stool she was standing on, bumping her elbow. A silent cry erupted, and I stopped the call.

I sat beside her on the kitchen floor. She was laughing again after getting an Octonauts Band-Aid and a popsicle from the freezer. As I looked into those brilliant eyes, my fury subsided. I recalled the final lines I'd delivered as Haley. It is a magical spot. I have seen the magic in your eyes. There is only one Tree Hill, and it's your home. I wanted Rosie to experience that kind of magic and peace. I had her. I had her. Nothing else mattered. I called my lawyer.

"I apologize, Joy. It's a difficult pill to swallow.

"It is fine. "I have nothing left to protect except her," I responded. "Sign it."

Made in the USA
Middletown, DE
28 January 2025